How to Write a
Thesis

5th edition

Harry Teitelbaum

THOMSON
ARCO

Australia • Canada • Mexico • Singapore • Spain • United Kingdom • United States

Contents

Preface

You have resolved that this term is going to be different. No more waiting until the long recess to sit down and write those papers due in English 205, Education 129, and Psychology 301. No more ruining vacations with endless hours spent in the library competing with all the other students who also waited until the last moment. No more scissors-and-paste projects, taking a little from this source and a little from that source and pasting them together with transitional paragraphs. This term you are going to approach your thesis paper systematically, so that the paper will have some meaning for you.

This book is dedicated to help you achieve your goal. Whether this is your first or fiftieth paper, the chapters that follow take you, step by step, from the selection and limitation of a topic to the final manuscript that you submit to your instructor. Its focus is not on content, but rather on the mechanical aspects of preparing the paper itself. It is a handy reference guide.

Be aware, however, that there are many different acceptable formats for a thesis paper. To avoid confusion, the text focuses on one form; additional forms are given in the Appendix. In the final analysis, however, it is your instructor or adviser who will determine the preferred format and it is this format that you will have to follow.

Since the organization and actual writing of the thesis paper are so closely related to that of the shorter essay, a chapter dealing with the necessary steps in writing a shorter theme—from topic selection and limitation to the writing of the final manuscript—has been added. This chapter should be of particular value to those students who have been experiencing difficulties in expressing themselves coherently and clearly.

Chapter One

The Thesis Paper vs. the Research Paper

The thesis paper has become so much a part of the academic scene that students often lose sight of its primary function. Contrary to what many think, it is not meant to torture students and ruin their vacations, nor is it a necessary evil accompanying college courses. The thesis paper, when carefully assigned and conscientiously done, has definite value.

Unfortunately, these two terms have been used interchangeably all too often. However, they are not synonymous. Although all research papers may well be *thesis* papers, all thesis papers do not necessarily require research.

The thesis paper is usually a paper assigned as a major part of the course requirement. If it does not require the use of outside sources, laboratory experimentation, or questionnaire analysis, then it is not a research paper. It is, then, generally a paper that may require a student to do some original thinking or evaluation. In English, for instance, it might be the close study of a text or the writing of a short story or simply a summary of some outside reading.

The research paper, on the other hand, is quite different. It requires the utilization of outside sources, laboratory experimentation, statistical analysis, and any and all other means that will enable the researcher to find the solution to the problem that she has set for herself and to present this knowledge in a well-written, coherent paper.

WHY RESEARCH PAPERS?

Ideally, the researched thesis paper is supposed to make one an authority on some area of an overall topic. Hence, it should incorporate an exhaustive search of any material that has been written on this given topic. Furthermore, the research should only be undertaken by the student who has already shown some interest in the subject. Unfortunately, this cannot always be achieved.

Since classroom time is limited and only so much information can be disseminated during one semester, the researched thesis paper affords students the wonderful opportunity to gain knowledge in different aspects of the subject being studied. It enables students to move into tangential areas, to increase knowledge, to sharpen insights, and to make new discoveries.

The researched thesis paper does afford unlimited opportunities to students—but only if approached properly. Anything that is hastily thrown together and that relies on secondary sources will be nothing more than an exercise in penmanship and a total waste of time.

Furthermore, the values of the researched thesis paper are, of course, not limited to the college classroom. They are an essential part of humanity's continuing desire to gain insight into and an understanding of the world. If the true purpose of higher education is to make one a better and more understanding person, then students must be given the tools with which they can continue to reach toward this ideal. Whether a college student is planning a career in medicine, science, education, or diplomacy, the ability to conduct original research will stand him in good stead. It will enable him to make important contributions to his profession, to humanity, and to himself. Research is certainly one of the important tools of an educated person.

TYPES OF RESEARCH

Research generally falls into two categories, *library* and *experimental*. Although these are by no means mutually exclusive, the first type of research is one in which no experimental design is set up, where information is obtained primarily from a search of written materials. The latter is primarily a "laboratory" study.

Library Research

Library research requires a search of written materials. This search is usually limited to books and articles that are readily available in the library. For the preparation of theses and dissertations, the search focuses on primary sources and requires a thorough search of all sources that might contain information about the chosen topic. Furthermore, the researcher may well have to become a sleuth, tracking down any and all leads, such as church and civil records, property transactions, personal correspondence, and even archaeological excavations.

Experimental Research

On the other hand, the experimental study uses a somewhat different approach. Surely, the library is still a very important avenue for this type of research, since it is in the library where you will be able to determine what has been found on the proposed subject. Aside from this and the gathering of general background information, the experimental paper focuses more on experimentation and/or observation. You must first prepare a statement of problems to be solved, and then set up an experimental design where you will create your control and experimental groups. This holds true whether the research is being conducted in either the social or physical sciences. Based on a careful record of your observations, you will then analyze the data, statistically if possible, and draw conclusions.

Incorporated into the experimental study may be the use of the questionnaire. Admittedly, there are serious drawbacks to a questionnaire study, including the inability to properly validate the responses. However, where adequate and carefully selected samplings are used, where questions are constructed and phrased with care, and, most importantly, where responses are analyzed by qualified personnel, these drawbacks may be minimized. Furthermore, with the advent of e-mail, the questionnaire study has become a much more practical and valid approach.

It must be stressed that these approaches are not mutually exclusive, nor is one always better than the other. The method that will enable you to find the answers to the problem that you have set for yourself is the best, as long as the results can be validated.

FINDING THE RIGHT TOPIC

One of the major problems confronting students is what to research. If possible, you should choose a topic in which you are interested—at least one that seems to hold the promise of being beneficial to you. This is not to say, of course, that you should shy away from anything that is not in the immediate realm of your knowledge or experience. On the contrary, the researched term paper will offer you the opportunity to explore new areas. But there must be at least some glimmer of interest on your part, for nothing can be more boring than spending months on a subject in which you have no interest.

Furthermore, there must be some purpose and use for the research. Research for its own sake cannot be justified under any conditions. It seems that much that passes for research today serves no other function than to fill up pages. The research must make a definite contribution, if not to the general body of knowledge, at least to the knowledge of the researcher.

HOW DO I LIMIT MY TOPIC?

Once the topic has been selected, it must be limited so that it can be treated thoroughly and in depth. Before limiting a topic, however, you must be aware of several factors that will affect the limitation—word limitation, preparation time, library facilities, audience. Let's look at each of these individually.

The audience—the readers for whom the paper is being written—plays an important role in the limitation and treatment of the topic. You should not assume that the paper is being written for the sole benefit of the instructor and simply to pass the course. If this were the basic assumption under which you worked, then the fruits of your research would be rather limited. You must know something about your potential audience, including:

- *How knowledgeable are they about this topic?*
- *How old are the members of the audience?*
- *What is their education level?*
- *Is the research being written for possible inclusion in a professional journal or in a lay magazine?*

Answers to these and other questions will certainly affect not only the topic limitation but also your treatment of the material. Certainly, you will not want to concern yourself with something highly technical if your audience consists of lay people with only a passing interest in the topic.

Perhaps of greater importance is the word limitation. Certainly justice cannot be done to a treatment of Mark Twain's cynicism or the development of the short story in America within the confines of a 2,000- to 3,000-word paper. These topics would require book-length treatment. You must remember that research demands more than a cursory, superficial treatment of a subject; the treatment must be thorough and in-depth.

The availability of material and the extensiveness of library facilities are also important factors to consider before limiting the topic. If you attend a small college with limited library resources, you cannot hope to undertake the same kind of research as a student at a major university—unless, of course, you are willing and have the time and the means to travel to those libraries where the material is available. Students in large cities like New York have another advantage since library facilities are rather extensive.

Amount of time for the preparation and submission of the final draft is another important factor to consider. All other things being equal, the student who has six months to prepare a paper is expected to do a more intensive and extensive job than the one with six weeks. Certainly the more time you have to prepare, the more wide-ranging your search can be. Here, the opportunity exists for utilizing library facilities outside the immediate area, for possible communication with potential sources, and for wider reading.

All of these factors must be taken into account before you can make an intelligent choice and limit your topic appropriately. However, there is another matter to be considered before this can be achieved and the library search begun. You must have some general knowledge of the broad topic you have chosen. In order to gain this knowledge, you must do some background reading. Here, a good general source book may be of help. You should browse through the library, check the card catalog, and look in the encyclopedia. Any or all of these will give you some valuable insight into the topic.

The topic is now ready to be limited to something that can be dealt with adequately and in-depth within the given restrictions. However, limitations cannot be arbitrary. There must be some valid reason for them. For example, you cannot just choose to study the short story from 1899 to 1910 unless you can justify the time limits. Nor can you choose to study Twain's pessimism in "The Man That Corrupted Hadleyburg" and "The Mysterious Stranger" unless you can justify the choice of these two stories. Limitations cannot be haphazard and artificial

Here's one final thought about topic limitations. Until a library search has been completed, any limitation is tentative and subject to change. Primarily, if you find a book dealing with the topic in terms of the limitations you have placed on it, you should not continue with the proposed research. For, at best, you would be presenting no more than a critical review of the text. Secondly, if your library search reveals that there is insufficient information available on your topic, you may need to broaden the topic again. Also, if there is too much material available to be adequately dealt with within the word limitation, then you need to limit the topic even further.

Once you have decided, based on the aforementioned criteria, on your limited topic and discussed it with your instructor, you are now ready to proceed with the next step in the preparation of a researched thesis paper—the library search.

Chapter Two

The Library Search

Before you can actually do any research, you must become familiar with the library facilities available to you. This does not include only the campus library but the libraries in and around the community. For example, you should ask:

- *How extensive are the collections in the community library?*
- *What are the library's hours of operation?*
- *Will I be permitted to make use of its resources?*
- *Is the local library a member of an interlibrary loan association that makes material that is not available locally accessible through one of its member branches?*

As far as the college library is concerned, you should become thoroughly familiar with its organization and content before undertaking any research, since it is here, in all probability, that you will be doing the greatest portion of your work. At most colleges, a tour of the library is part of the freshman English curriculum. If, on the other hand, you are not so fortunate, you must take it upon yourself to become acquainted with the library and its resources.

First, you must locate various reference materials in the library—the card catalog, reserve reading room, periodical collection, general reference materials, vertical file, stacks, information desk, loan desk, special collections, computer terminals, and copying machines.

Second, you should acquaint yourself with the library rules and regulations. For example:

- *Are undergraduates allowed to use the stacks collection?*
- *What is the time limit for the loan of books on reserve?*
- *Which periodicals are in circulation?*

Third, a cursory inspection of the size of the library, the periodicals to which it subscribes, its special collection, and the friendliness of its staff can very often give you insight into the extensiveness of the facilities and the pleasantness of the surroundings. Both of these—although the former is by far the more important—are important adjuncts to successful research.

Now let's take a closer look at some of the resources you will be using.

CARD CATALOG

Holdings are indexed alphabetically in the card catalog; each work is catalogued under the author's last name, title, and subject. Each work is classified with a call number so it can be located quickly and easily. Although a thorough knowledge of the classification system is not necessary for the average student, an awareness of the method used by the library in which one works can be helpful. This is especially true in libraries where students are permitted to go into the stacks. They will then be able to find the classes of books in which they are interested without going to the card catalog.

There are two major methods of classification currently in use: the **Dewey Decimal system** and the **Library of Congress system.** The former is used by most libraries of average size, and the latter is used by the larger libraries, including most university libraries because of its greater flexibility.

The Dewey Decimal system divides books into ten classes, assigning each class 100 numbers:

000-099	General Works	500-599	Pure Science
100-199	Philosophy	600-699	Technology
200-299	Religion		(Useful Arts)
300-399	Social Sciences	700-799	Fine Arts
400-499	Language	800-899	Literature
	(Philology)	900-999	History

Each main class is further divided into ten subdivisions:

800	General Literature	850	Italian Literature
810	American Literature	860	Spanish Literature
820	English Literature	870	Latin Literature
830	German Literature	880	Greek Literature
840	French Literature	890	Minor Literature

Each of these divisions is again subdivided into ten groups:

820	English Literature	825	English oratory
821	English poetry	826	English letters
822	English drama	827	English satire
823	English fiction	828	English miscellany
824	English essays	829	Anglo-Saxon

Further subdivisions are indicated by decimals where each decimal unit indicates another breakdown of the general topic. Added to this is a book or author number that enables the library to distinguish the many books in any one classification. The book number consists of the initial of the author's last name plus a series of numbers.

The Library of Congress system, originally devised for classifying the holdings of the Library of Congress, is a more flexible classification system and is, therefore, used by libraries that have large holdings. This system divides books into twenty main groups, assigning a letter to each:

A	General Work	L	Education
B	Philosophy—Religion	M	Music
C	History—Auxiliary Sciences	N	Fine Arts
		P	Language and Literature
D	Foreign History and Topography	Q	Science
E	American History	R	Medicine
F	American History	S	Agriculture
G	Geography—Anthropology	T	Technology
		U	Military Science
H	Social Sciences	V	Naval Science
J	Political Science	Z	Bibliography—Library Science
K	Law		

This system then combines additional letters and Arabic numerals for subdivisions and to show the call number of a specific work. Since the combination of letters and numbers is almost without limit, the Library of Congress system is preferred by larger libraries.

Once the library holdings have been classified, the cards are indexed in the card catalog files. For most books there will be at least three cards: the **author** card (*see page 10*), the **title** card (*see page 11*), and at least one **subject** card (*see page 11*).

1. *ML 200.5. T5* is the number of the book. This library uses the Library of Congress classification system.

2. *Thomson, Virgil 1896—* is the name of the author and the year of his birth. In those cases where the author had died prior to the time that the card was printed, the year of birth will be followed by the year of death.

3. *American . . . 1910* is the full title of the book, place of publication, publishing company, and year of publication. In this instance, the work also contains an introduction to the text. The student should note that the library practice of capitalizing titles differs from general practice.

4. *xvi . . . 23* cm. specifies that the book contains 16 introductory pages and 204 pages of text, that there are illustrations, facsimiles, music, and portraits, and that the book is 23 centimeters (2.54 cm. 5.1 inch) high.

Author card

```
ML 200.5
  T5   Thomson, Virgil, 1896 –
            American music since 1910. With an introd. by
       Nicolas Nabokov. New York, Holt, Rinehart and
       Winston, 1971.
       xvi, 204 p. illus., facsims., music, ports., 23 cm.
       Bibliography: p. 187 – 189.
       CONTENTS.—America's musical maturity.—American mu-
       sical traits.—The Ives case.—Ruggles.—Varese.—Aaron Cop-
       land.—Looking backward.—Cage and the collage of noises.—
       Let us now praise famous men.—The operas of Virgil Thom-
       son, by V. F. Yellin.—Music in Latin America, by G. Chase.—
       106 American composers.
            1. Music, American — History and criticism. 2. Music
       —History and criticism — 20th century. 3. Composers,
       American — Biography. I. Title.
       ML200.5.T5                      780.973          SCLS 2767-25
       Library of Congress            ⌐5⌐
```

5. *Bibliography: p. 187-189* indicates that the bibliography begins on page 187 and ends on page 189. This information can be extremely helpful when preparing one's own working bibliography by suggesting additional sources.

6. *CONTENTS . . . composers* indicates the table of contents of the book. Some cards may also contain a quotation from the title page of the book or a brief synopsis of the highlights of the work.

7. *1. Music . . . L Title* specifies that this book is also listed under three subject headings: (1) Music, under the subdivision American, and under the further subdivision *History and criticism,* (2) *Music,* under the subdivision *History and criticism, 20th century,* and (3) *Composers,* under the subdivision *American, Biography*. These subject headings will suggest other headings where the student can locate additional sources. The book is also indexed under the title. If the title begins with the article *a, an,* or *the,* then it is then alphabetized by the word following the article. This book, then, has five cards in the card catalog.

8. *ML 200.5. T5* is the Library of Congress call number.

9. *780.973* is the Dewey system call number.

10. *SCLS 2767-25* is the order number for the card.

11. *Library of Congress* indicates that a copy of this work is shelved in and catalogued by the Library of Congress.

12. *5* is the printer's key.

Title card

> ML 200.5 American music since 1910
>   T5   **Thomson, Virgil,** 1896 –
>
> American music since 1910. With an introd. by Nicolas Nabokov. New York . . .

With the exception of the title of the book typed above the author's name, the title card is an exact duplicate of the author card.

Subject card

> ML 200.5 MUSIC—HISTORY AND CRITICISM—20th
>   T5   CENTURY
>   **Thomson, Virgil,** 1896 –
>
> American music since 1910. With an introd. by Nicolas Nabokov. New York . . .

The subject card is also an exact duplicate of the author card, except that the subject heading is typed above the author's name in uppercase letters.

A thorough understanding of the contents of the card catalog and a careful perusal of the card can be a valuable time-saver when doing research. Information about whether or not the book contains a bibliography, illustrations, tables, maps, introduction, or portraits can be used to good advantage. Furthermore, the subject headings at the bottom of the card give a good clue about where to look for more information on the topic. You should be aware, however, that in recent years many libraries have eliminated the card catalog file and have computerized their holdings. The use of computer terminals is discussed later in this chapter.

GENERAL INDEXES

The card catalog, as mentioned earlier, limits itself solely to titles of books that the library has in its collection. It does not list titles of the individual articles, essays, or short stories within the books or appearing in periodicals. These are indexed in a variety of sources. Here are some of the more common ones:

- *Reader's Guide to Periodical Literature,* 1960 to date, published semimonthly from September to June and monthly during July and August and bound at the end of each year in one volume. The *Reader's Guide* indexes articles appearing in approximately 100 magazines under subject, author, and title.
- *Poole's Index to Periodical Literature,* from 1802 through January 1, 1907. Articles appearing in American and English periodicals are indexed mainly by subject.
- *Essay and General Literature Index,* 1900 to date, published semiannually. Includes indexes, essays, and articles appearing in collections by author, title, and subject.
- *Short Story Index,* 1989-1993, lists short stories appearing in collections under author, title, and subject.
- *Granger's Index to Poetry and Recitations* indexes poems appearing in collections by author, title, subject, and first line of the poem.

In addition to these general indexes, there are a multitude of indexes for special subjects or countries. Among these are *Agricultural Index, Applied Science and Technology Index, The Art Index, Business Periodicals Index, Dramatic Index, The Education Index, Engineering Index, Index to Legal Periodicals, International Index to Periodicals, The New York Times Index, Index to One-Act Plays, Index to Speeches, Public Affairs Information Index,* and *Industrial Arts Index.*

Before using any index, it would be wise to take a few moments to read the introductory pages of the index under consideration. Here, you find explicit instructions on how the index has been organized. Also, it must be noted that simply because a work is indexed is no indication that the library has it in its holdings. However, each library does have a card file, usually in the Periodicals Room, that lists the titles of magazines and the inclusive volumes and dates that it has. Larger libraries list their holdings on microfiche containing titles of the periodicals and call numbers of the bound editions. These microfiches can be read through the use of a special machine that magnifies them and is relatively easy to use. Also, back issues of newspapers and frequently used periodicals may be stored on microforms (microfilm, microcard, or microfiche) to conserve space. Current issues of magazines are usually on open shelves; past issues are bound in volumes and shelved in the stacks. In most cases, magazines and newspapers are not circulated but must be read in the library.

USING COMPUTER TERMINALS FOR RESEARCH

Most, if not all, libraries have computer terminals with access to various databases, making the library search much easier and faster. Here, again, it is imperative that you first become familiar with the databases available, the procedure to be followed, and any limitations imposed by the library. Here are some of the databases currently used:

MELVYL System

Materials can be accessed through title, author, and subject searches. Periodicals can also be located by title. Other MELVYL Indexes include Medline (a current five-year index to articles in medical journals), *Current Contents* (index to current periodical literature from over 6,700 periodicals), *Current Contents Table of Contents* (tables of contents for current journals), and *Mags* (index of articles from 1,000 journals and magazines).

InfoTrac

This system has various indexes that can be accessed. The *Info Trac Magazine Index* offers full-text news articles and features from more than 300 publications. The *New York Times* offers evaluations of consumer products, provides graded reviews of books, movies, hotels, etc., and tracks social and economic trends. *Info Trac National Newspaper Index* indexes the *New York Times, Los Angeles Times, The Wall Street Journal, Christian Science Monitor,* and the *Washington Post. Info Trac Academic Index* covers 500 scholarly and general interest magazines in the humanities, social sciences, and general sciences. *ProQuest Index* lists indexes and contains abstracts of 130 current interest periodicals, including the *New York Times* and *USA Today. Social Issues Resources Series Index* contains thousands of articles about the social and general sciences from magazines, newspapers, and government documents.

There are more than 250 databases and search capabilities available. Some of the other programs, such as the Educational Resources Information Center (ERIC), supply not only the bibliographic references but also copies of the documents for a fee. In addition, many libraries have access to most libraries in the United States and Canada through Inter-Library Loan and can obtain the necessary materials quickly and inexpensively.

It's imperative that you familiarize yourself with the programs used in libraries. Carefully read the material prepared by them on the proper use of computer terminals, follow the directions on the computer, and never hesitate to ask the librarian for help. For more detailed information on online research, students should consult:

REFERENCE BOOKS

Just as knowledge of the use of the card catalog and indexes is an invaluable aid in conducting research, an awareness of the reference materials available is necessary before any research can be completed. Usually the investigation of a topic begins with trying to get an overview of the broad topic. This is most readily done by reading articles in reference works.

Before beginning research, familiarize yourself with the types of reference works available and their basic organization. A few moments spent in the careful reading of the introductory material will familiarize you with the work's scheme of headings, cross-references, and abbreviations. You will also learn whether the articles are signed, if the work is geared for the layman or the professional, whether it contains bibliographical listings and other references, how many volumes there are, if there is a general index volume, and if there have been any supplements. This preliminary check will also enable you to note the date of publication, which is especially important if you are researching a topic where new developments are constantly taking place. The date should indicate immediately whether the work will be of any value. Whenever you are in doubt about the value of the reference work, never hesitate to check with the reference librarian.

Reference books can be categorized according to the function they serve and according to their content:

1. Encyclopedias—general and specific
2. Dictionaries and word books
3. Handbooks and yearbooks
4. Atlases
5. Books of quotations
6. Biographical dictionaries
7. Bibliographies
8. Standard works basic to any subject area, which sometimes are circulated.
9. Indexes—general and special

In addition, you should check and thoroughly familiarize yourself with those references that are particularly pertinent to your subject.

RESERVE BOOKS

College libraries, as a rule, have a number of books on reserve—that is, not available for general circulation. In order to assure their availability, books may be placed on reserve for students in a particular department or for a certain instructor's class. Books that are on reserve can readily be identified in the card catalog. The cards of these books are "tagged" with a clip, with an insert card marked "reserved," with a cellophane envelope marked "reserved," or in some other manner determined by the library. When a book is placed on reserve, it is removed from the stacks. You will generally find an index listing all the books currently on reserve in a room specially set aside for them. Reserve books may be restricted to library use only or may be placed in limited circulation, ranging from overnight to seventy-two hours. To ensure their prompt return, libraries usually impose a heavy fine for overdue reserve books.

EVALUATING SOURCES

A printed source does not necessarily mean a reliable one. Nor does the inclusion of a source in a library's holdings attest to its reliability. Hence, it becomes imperative that before you make use of any sources in the preparation of your paper, you evaluate the reliability of the materials.

All encyclopedias are not equally reliable. Those prepared for elementary or secondary school students generally are superficial in their presentation of the material. This is equally true of encyclopedias sold in supermarkets and discount stores. Before using any encyclopedia, you should check the age group to which it is geared, the date of its most recent revision, and, if possible, the reliability and qualifications of its editors.

Also, although the reference works listed in Sheehy's and Winchell's texts will be reliable, the degree of reliability will vary depending on your purpose. Some of these sources will vary in the degree of coverage, and, therefore, although the information may be accurate, all the facts may not be included.

It will be more difficult to ascertain the reliability of the books, articles, and essays that you select from the various indexes. However, you can use the following checklist as a guide:

1. **The author:** The author's reputation is the best criterion for judging the reliability of a source. If she is well known and respected in her field, you can rest assured that the work has merit. But an authority, say, on military strategy is not necessarily an authority on poetry. When in doubt, you should

check the writer's qualifications in a biographical dictionary. Very often, however, the author's qualifications are listed on the title page or in the introduction.

2. **The publisher:** The more established and well known the publisher, the less likely it will be to publish unreliable works. If you find that the publishing firm listed on the copyright page is not known, then you should question the reliability of the text. Certainly, if no publisher is listed, or if the book has been published privately, you have every right to be skeptical.

3. **Date of publication:** The year in which the book was published is indicated on the bottom of the title page. This is especially important when researching a topic where there are constantly new developments. The more recent the date of publication, the more up-to-date the content. This is a good time to call your attention to the difference between numbered printings, numbered editions, and revised editions. Of these three, a *numbered printing* indicates no changes whatsoever in the text. It simply means that the book has been reprinted, usually using the original data. A *numbered edition* indicates some changes in the text, more in the format than in the actual content. A *revised edition* indicates changes in the content and format; the extent of the changes, however, can only be determined by a comparison of the new edition with the old, or by statements made in the preface.

4. **Periodicals:** The type of magazine in which an article appears and the audience for whom it is intended are important criteria in the evaluation of published articles. Generally, the more technical or scholarly the magazine, the more reliable the articles. This, of course, is not to say that reliable articles will not appear in the popular magazines. However, the treatment of the subject will probably be more superficial since it is geared toward the general public. In the evaluation of magazine articles, you should take into account the criteria established for authors. Unsigned articles should be evaluated carefully. The lack of an author's credit does not necessarily cast doubt on the worth of the material. There are some periodicals, especially English ones, that maintain anonymity in authorship as a matter of policy. On the other hand, unsigned articles in popular magazines should be read very critically.

5. **Content:** A cursory inspection of the book—preface, introduction, index, footnotes, bibliography, and appendices—give some clue to its reliability. In addition, spot reading will reveal whether the writer is objective or emotional; whether the writer tends to substantiate opinions and arguments with facts and with cross-references to other works; and whether the tone is impartial, analytical, cynical, or sarcastic.

Chapter Three

The Working Bibliography

Okay, you have done some reading in general or special reference sources to familiarize yourself with your subject. Based on this, and following the procedures outlined in chapter one, you have limited your topic accordingly. In addition, you have spent sufficient time familiarizing yourself with the library resources so that from here on your research will not be hampered by strange surroundings. It is at this point that you are ready to begin making use of your knowledge of the library and begin preparing your bibliography.

REASONS FOR A WORKING BIBLIOGRAPHY

Since research implies a thorough search of all available sources on a given topic, it is imperative that you undertake a very careful and systematic search of the available sources and keep an orderly record of the search. This search cannot be a haphazard affair. The more organized you are from the start, the more time you will save by avoiding unnecessary delay and repetition.

The working bibliography is just what the name implies—the bibliography that you will be working with until your final draft has been submitted and accepted. In a sense, a working bibliography is never really completed, since at any time during the general preparation and taking of notes you might discover additional sources that you will then add to your bibliography file.

PROCEDURE

Before doing anything else, you must purchase a pack of 3×5 index cards. Index cards are recommended rather than slips of paper because they will hold up better over a longer period of time and under repeated handling. In addition, you must resolve to take your time in making entries on these cards. Always make the entries in ink (pencil tends to smudge). Never make hasty entries on tear-off pages and the back of books, even though you have every intention of copying these neatly "later." Unfortunately, many of these resolutions, well-intentioned though they are, fall by the wayside.

With the topic clearly limited and with full awareness of what aspect of the topic you are focusing on, you are now ready to begin your search. It is at this time that you will begin making practical use of many of the indexes and reference sources discussed in the previous chapter. For each source that seems to hold promise—based on the title, on the annotation, on the comment on the card in the catalog—you should prepare a separate bibliography card. The card should include the author's name, the title of the work, the place of publication, publisher, and date of publication. This information should always be checked against the actual title page of the book before the bibliography is finalized. The cards should also include the call number, the library in which the work has been located, and, after the work has been checked, some terse comment concerning its potential worth.

You must be careful not to overlook any potential sources of information. To be sure, a card catalog is the most popular and the most frequently used. But any research paper based solely on the works located in the card catalog is not valid research. A wealth of information can be found in periodicals, in introductions to collections and texts, and in unpublished manuscripts, most notably masters' theses and doctoral dissertations.[1]

Having compiled your working bibliography, you probably have a sizeable file of titles that might contain some pertinent information on your topic. Perhaps it should be pointed out again that, in all probability, none of these works will deal entirely with your topic as you have narrowed it. If any of them should, there would be no need for you to research the topic. It would have already been done.

You might find it helpful to organize your bibliography cards so you can check the sources easily. All essays and articles from periodicals should be filed in one group that could then be separated according to periodical, all general reference sources filed in another group, and all general circulation works separated according to call number. Of course, any method you find least time-consuming and most helpful is the best.

The next step is to check each of these sources and make a cursory inspection of the work. Incorporated in this inspection will be an analysis of the reliability of the

---

[1] Masters' theses can be found indexed in *Guide to Bibliographies of Theses, U. S. and Canada*, and doctoral dissertations in *Doctoral Dissertations Accepted by American Universities*. Although most colleges and universities have abstracts of the doctoral dissertations indexed (usually on microfilm), the dissertation itself is somewhat harder to obtain, unless it was submitted to the university where the student is doing his own research. However, copies of the dissertations can be obtained by applying to the granting university and paying a prescribed fee.

work, using the criteria established in the previous chapter; a check of the table of contents, index, style and tone, and bibliography, which might well mean additional bibliography cards for the working bibliography; graphs, tables, and preface. Based on this, you will make some appropriate comment on your card concerning the work's worth. Comments may range from "no good" to "excellent bibliography" to "highly subjective." You should make appropriate comments that will recall your reactions at a later date. You should *not* begin reading through your sources and taking notes at this time.

Once all sources have been checked, the cards should then be filed alphabetically by author's last name (if there is no author, by first word of the title exclusive of articles), and numbered consecutively with Arabic numerals in the upper right-hand corner. Under no circumstances should any card be destroyed or discarded at this time.

Even though a work, after the check, is totally irrelevant and has been marked "NG (no good)," the card should be retained for one very simple reason. Months down the road, while you are embroiled in your reading and note taking, you might come across the title of a source that seems to hold great promise. You decide to get the work, but find that it is currently unavailable. You put in a call for it and, after several weeks of waiting anxiously, finally get the coveted work—only to discover that it was the same work that you had checked out some months earlier and found irrelevant. Had you retained all of the bibliography cards, however, you could have checked your file and discovered immediately that the book had no merit. This would have saved a great deal of time and energy.

SAMPLE BIBLIOGRAPHY CARDS

Again, the neatness and orderliness of the cards must be stressed. You should decide on a format and use it consistently, varying it as little as possible. Here are three sample entries: full-length work, an essay from a collection, and an article from a periodical.

Book by one author[2]

Aside from the bibliographic information, this card contains the call number of the book, the library in which the book has been located ("HU"—Hofstra University; you should devise your own system to identify the location of the source), a comment concerning the value of the book, a rating assigned by you ("A" in the lower right corner, meaning excellent; here again you should predetermine a ranking system), and the card number in the upper right corner ("26"—twenty-sixth card in the alphabetical arrangement of the bibliography cards by author's last name. This number will later be used as a reference number on the note cards to identify the source of the notes.).

---

[2] The basic form of the bibliography card will remain the same for all entries; the only variation will occur in the bibliographic entry. For all possible variations in that, see Chapter Nine, pp. 71-76.

Essay from a collection

> McLuhan, Marshall.
>   "Blondie," The Art of the Essay.
>   2d ed. Ed. by Leslie Fiedler. New
>   York: Thomas Y. Crowell Company,
>   1969. Pp. 489–493.
>
> Pers. lit.   Not pertinent to topic.
>   NG   (D)
>
> (18)

The general format of the card is the same, but there are variations in the entry. The title of the essay is placed in quotation marks, the title of the work in which it appears is underlined (italicized), and the pages on which the essay appears are listed. As this book is located in your personal library, no call number is indicated. Since this book is not relevant, it has been rated "D." In the ranking schedule established here, A=excellent source, B=pertinent information but very limited, C=interesting but totally subjective or of questionable reliability, and D=not pertinent.

Article from a periodical

> Lund, T. A.
>   "Grammar Should Be
>   Groovier," Education Digest,
>   34: 32–34. March, 1969.
>
> Local Lib.   Delightfully written —
>   some potential
>   (C)
>
> (16)

No call number is listed since periodicals do not have any. In the entry, "34:32-34," the number before the colon is the volume number; those following are the page numbers. The periodical is located in the local community library.

You are again reminded of the importance of making all entries as indicated and making them very carefully. Although this may be more time consuming at the moment, it will save untold hours later on. Such information as the call number and the library where the source is located, plus legibility and neatness, will preclude the necessity of checking the card catalog or other indexes again. With all this in mind, you should be able to prepare a working bibliography that will be a constant aid to you in your research.

Chapter Four

Note Taking

With the completion of the working bibliography, the bulk of the library work has been completed. You now know what sources are available and where they are located. There should be no need, for the most part, for you to make use of reference sources and indexes again. You are now ready to begin reading and taking notes.

At this point you might be tempted to take copious notes as you read a book or an article and to leave the worries about organization and the writing of the paper until later. The tendency is to supply yourself with a pad of legal-size, lined yellow paper; write industriously on every line on both sides, usually in pencil; and to conserve time, make frequent use of abbreviations, making them up as you proceed. Although this seems to be the shortest and easiest way, it will prove to be the most time-consuming and frustrating method in the long run. Proper research and note-taking procedures must begin with a statement of thesis and a tentative outline.

THESIS STATEMENT

From your preliminary reading, from examination of the sources in the preparation of your working bibliography, from discussing the topic with your instructor or adviser, and from thinking about the subject, you should be able to formulate a thesis statement, or the statement of the problem. This statement will enable you to focus your plan of attack and aid you in outlining your paper. It is the controlling factor or the focal point around which your research will revolve. It will force you to clarify your thinking and to determine what is relevant and irrelevant in your reading. It will eliminate the tendency to take endless notes that will have no bearing on your primary objective.

The thesis statement must be written down after careful deliberation and polished until it finally encompasses the central idea. Usually, it is stated in the form of a problem that you hope to resolve through your research, since a thesis statement technically is a statement of the solution. In research, the thesis is the anticipated result that you will either validate or invalidate.

Assume you are researching the writings of Stephen Crane. After preliminary reading, you may have limited the topic to "Crane as a naturalistic writer," and further limited it to "naturalism in *The Red Badge of Courage*." Since you are beginning to research your topic, you are not yet certain that the book is naturalistic. Thus, your problem is to determine if there are indications of naturalistic philosophy in the work and, if so, what they are. You would then formulate your thesis statement along these lines:

Statement of the problem: To determine what aspects of naturalism are inherent in Stephen Crane's *The Red Badge of Courage*.

Although your own lack of knowledge might require some careful and detailed reading on naturalism, it is not a necessary adjunct to the paper. According to the thesis statement, the paper will limit itself to the aspects of naturalism found in the book. This will be your guideline, one that you will have to refer to frequently in the preparation of your preliminary outline, for anything that does not contribute to proving that statement is irrelevant, regardless of how interesting it may be. Hence, references to the biography of the author, other naturalistic writers, and the origin of the naturalistic school are all irrelevant.

Let us look at another possible topic. Let's say you have decided to write about "the extrinsic factors in the interpretation of poetry." Through your preliminary reading, you may have limited your topic to "the possible effect of biography in the interpretation of selected sonnets by Elizabeth Barrett Browning." You would then formulate your thesis statement as follows:

Statement of the problem: To determine what effect a knowledge of Elizabeth Browning's courtship with Robert Browning has on the interpretation of her sonnets.

There is, of course, nothing final about the thesis statement. It may be modified as you become more deeply embroiled in your research. You may discover, for example, that the topic needs to be limited further or broadened.

PRELIMINARY OUTLINE

If your reading and note taking are to have any direction and if you are able to exercise any discretion in what you do and do not write down, you must draw up some plan that will act as a blueprint. This blueprint is your preliminary outline. Perhaps it might be more appropriate to call this a preliminary "tentative" outline, for such an outline is, of course, subject to change as you do more reading and become more familiar with the subject under investigation. Here again, the outline is not permanent until the paper has been written. However, proper care in the preparation of this outline will require a minimum of changes later, and the fewer changes, the less time you'll spend needlessly reading, note taking, and revising.

Preliminary outlining is an organizational process. You should put your thoughts down on paper with the idea that you will be reviewing this outline and eliminating items that are not pertinent. At this point, it is not imperative that you follow the formal Harvard outline format, although using it will probably help you to organize your thoughts more logically. The organization may follow a chronological, logical, or cause-and-effect order, to name a few. The actual order will be determined by the subject matter.

Always keeping your thesis statement before you, you should list those topics that you think should be discussed in your paper. After listing all possible topics, you should check each one against your thesis statement, asking yourself, "Will this help to prove my thesis?" If the answer is no, then that topic should be eliminated. The remaining topics should be organized in a logical order, focused on solving the problem set forth in the thesis statement. This order should incorporate major divisions, indicated with Roman numerals, and subdivisions, indicated with capital letters and Arabic numerals.

The outline for the proposed paper on naturalism in *The Red Badge of Courage* might look something like this:

NATURALISM IN *THE RED BADGE OF COURAGE*

Preliminary Outline

Thesis Statement: To determine what aspects of naturalism are inherent in Stephen Crane's *Red Badge of Courage*.

I. **Naturalism**
 A. Brief definition
 B. Major tenets
 C. Relation to literature

II. **Importance of details in naturalistic writings**

III. **Tone of naturalism**
 A. In philosophy
 B. In *Red Badge* . . .

IV. **Evidences of naturalistic thought in *Red Badge* . . .**
 A. Animalistic behavior
 B. Survival—self-preservation
 C. Effect of heredity on behavior
 D. Effect of environment on behavior
 E. Obsession with violence

V. **Theme of *Red Badge* . . .**

This, of course, is not the first outline you would have done, nor is it the last before the paper is finally completed. Although each of the items here tends to substantiate the thesis statement and is pertinent, changes have to be made to reflect greater insight gained as the reading progresses.

NOTE CARD FORMAT

With the preliminary outline prepared, you are now ready to begin your reading. Armed with your working bibliography, you are ready to approach your reading and note taking systematically. Since your cards contain comments and ratings, you can be selective about which works you will read first. However, first you must know something about proper note-taking procedures.

First, you need to purchase large-size index cards—4×6 or, better yet, 5×8—that you will carry with you whenever you are about to do any reading on your topic. This is an important habit to get into. You will find that, in the long run, standard-size cards are easier to handle than either notebooks or long sheets of paper. Here again, it might well require breaking the old habit of jotting down notes on whatever happens to be handy at the moment. Although this process of note taking will again seem to be more time consuming at the start, it will make the actual writing of the paper considerably easier.

Armed with your working bibliography and preliminary outline, it is time to approach your sources. It is the bibliography cards that determine which source you read, but it is your preliminary outline that determines what you will read in the source, and, more importantly, what you will write down. You should take your notes not by book, but in accordance with your preliminary outline. That is to say, from one source you might conceivably have as many cards as there are topics in your outline.

As you read and come to some relevant information on one of the topics from your outline, you will take a card and enter the following:

- *On the top line, the pertinent topic from the outline*
- *In the upper right corner, the source number from the bibliography card*
- *Following your notes, the page number or numbers where the information has been found*

Sample note cards

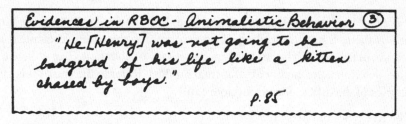

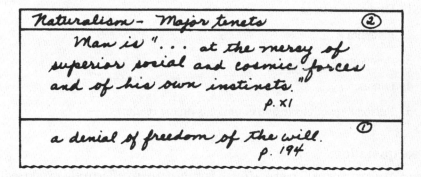

It should be noted that notes from more than one source may be entered on a single card. If the note from one source is rather brief, as it is on the second sample, then notes from another source may be added. It is important, though, that a line be drawn to separate the two sources and that the second source number be placed in the right corner.

Accuracy in note taking cannot be overemphasized. The omission of one small detail, such as the source number or the page number, may mean extra hours spent trying to obtain information that could readily have been gotten the first time. Although it is certainly permissible to write on both sides of the card, you will find it advantageous not to do so. You will find that having notes on one side only, especially when it comes to the actual writing of the paper, will facilitate the handling of the cards. All notes should be taken in ink since pencil will smudge. You should not type your notes—it is impractical and a waste of time.

TYPES OF NOTES

There are five basic types of notes you can take. It is imperative that you are familiar with all of them. Since the reading of your sources is the essential element in the preparation of the paper, it is the caliber and accuracy of your notes that will, to a great measure, determine the quality of your final product. Refer to the end of this chapter for samples of the different types of note cards.

The five types of notes are:

1. Direct quotations

2. Paraphrase

3. Précis and summary

4. Outline

5. Personal reactions to and comments on the readings

Direct quotations[1]

In your reading, you will come across ideas that are so effectively expressed that changing the wording would affect the impact of the statement. In addition, you may be impelled to quote where the meaning may be changed if you were to paraphrase. Be careful not to over quote and use lengthy quotations. These generally add little to the paper except monotony. A careful paraphrase that does justice to the source is preferable to a lengthy quotation.

As you are doing your reading, you must determine if the information warrants quoting. If in doubt, copy the item verbatim. You can always paraphrase it in your paper. Once you have decided to quote, you must exercise the greatest care to copy the original exactly, including any errors, and to place the entire statement in quotation marks. Since you will be quoting only part of a selection, you must also ensure that by taking the statement out of context you are not changing the basic meaning, tone, or intent of the author.

It is most important to remember to indicate the page number or numbers from which you quoted, since failure to acknowledge your source is considered plagiarism. If the quotation in the original source continues onto a second page, a slash (/) may be used to indicate the page division, although it is not necessary.

---

[1] For a detailed discussion of types of quotation and the mechanics of punctuation, see Chapter Seven, pp. 51-57.

Occasionally, you will find that the source you are using is quoting some other source. Although it is always best to go back to the primary source, there will be times when you must make use of this secondary source. In doing so, you must be sure to transcribe this quotation in single quotation marks and specify, in addition to the page number, the original source.

There are three particular problems that you might encounter when using quotations:

1. If there is some error in the quoted passage, *sic* (Latin for "thus") should be placed in brackets following the error to indicate that the error is in the original. However, the term should not be overused. Passages written in substandard English or in fifteenth-century English should not be strewn with *sic*s.

2. If there is some information you want to insert within the quoted matter, then you must place it within brackets, and the insertion must conform grammatically and structurally to the quotation. Parentheses may not be substituted for the brackets.

3. If there is some part of the quotation you want to omit, you may do so—as long as the omission does not affect the meaning or tone of the quotation—by indicating the ellipsis with three spaced dots (. . .).

Paraphrase

If the exact phrasing of the statement is not important, then the material should be paraphrased—restated in your own words. A paraphrased statement will be approximately the same length as the original. To avoid the possibility of using the author's words with some minor changes, you should carefully read the passage to be paraphrased, then close the text and write down the statement. Here, too, page numbers must be indicated. Even though the statement has not been quoted, the source must be acknowledged.

Précis and summary

The bulk of the notes will be in either précis or summary form. The précis is a condensation of the original (usually one-fourth to one-third of the length), retaining, for the most part, the author's style, tone, point of view, and, very frequently, her words. Illustrations, the detailed explanations, and anything else you can eliminate that will permit you to express the gist of the passage should be eliminated. The summary, on the other hand, is the gist of a passage stated in your own words with no attempt made to retain the original tone, style, or point of view.

You will find that since your research will not be limited to facts alone, but will incorporate ideas as well, you must be able to comprehend these ideas and incorporate them into your thinking. Taking copious notes is not the best way to accomplish this. It can be more effectively done by concentrating on the selection, laying the source aside, thinking the ideas through, and then writing the précis or summary. After the notes have been written, you should check them against the source to make sure the facts and ideas were not inadvertently misstated. Page numbers must be indicated just as for direct quotations and paraphrased statements.

Outline

In lieu of the summary, the outline, highlighting major ideas of a longer passage, may be used to good advantage. This form, however, should be used sparingly and when used should conform to correct outline format.

Personal reactions and comments

Since you will be relying solely on note cards when writing the paper, you will find it advantageous to jot down your personal comments and reactions to the information. This is highly recommended since it is best to write down one's reactions the moment they occur. No matter how strong the reaction is at the time, it might be difficult to recall months later. However, you must devise some method to distinguish your comments from the notes on the sources. Several possibilities exist, including the use of different color ink, printing your observations where all other notes are written in script, or boxing your comments. Any method works as long as it is readily distinguishable from the other notes and you use it consistently.

The reading of the sources and note taking are the most time-consuming—and most rewarding—parts of research. You should again exercise great care with this phase of your research. If you want to avoid duplication and possible charges of inaccuracy or plagiarism, then you must constantly be on the alert against carelessness and slovenliness. In addition, to ensure proper focus on your topic, you must check your preliminary outline for possible revision. Once you have completed taking notes, your research, for all intents and purposes, is complete. Nothing remains but the writing of your results.

SAMPLE TYPES OF NOTE CARDS

1. Sample Note card—Summary

```
 ┌────────────────────────────────────────┐
 │ Stephen Crane - Background          ⑥   │
 │    Received military instruction at his │
 │ prep school (Cloverack); he excelled in │
 │ it.                                     │
 │    Became acquainted with a General     │
 │ Van Patten. Stories told by General at  │
 │ the school may be similar to            │
 │ those of Henry F. in RBOC.              │
 │                                         │
 │                           pp. 1-2       │
 └────────────────────────────────────────┘
```

2. Sample Note card—Combination Paraphrase and Direct Quotation

```
 ┌────────────────────────────────────────┐
 │ Naturalism in RBOC - Animal Behavior ③ │
 │    Henry F. had no control over his     │
 │ actions; "... he could not flee, no     │
 │ more than a little finger can commit a  │
 │ revolution from a hand."     p.31       │
 │    A soldier who came from the lines    │
 │ before the enemy advanced was stopped   │
 │ and slapped repeatedly by the lt. The   │
 │ soldier "... stared with sheep-like     │
 │ eyes" and went back to the battle like  │
 │ "... a driven animal."                  │
 │                           p. 33         │
 └────────────────────────────────────────┘
```

3. Sample Note card—Direct Quotation with Personal Comment

> *Definition of Naturalism*   ②
>
> "Naturalism has implications that are pessimistic, irrationalist, and amoral since its technique is to break down into a shimmering flow of experience, the three dimensions that symbolized rationality and religious and social order in traditional art."   p. xii
>
> [possible use as concluding part of paper.]

4. Sample Note card—Outline Form

> *Naturalism in RBOC – Animal Behavior* ③
>
> Following are examples of animalistic behavior in RBOC:
>
> 1. like a proverbial chicken — p. 38
> 2. Henry, like "a pestered animal," "a cow carried by dogs." — p. 32
> 3. Armies fought "panther fashion." p. 44
> 4. Rage equal to that of "a driven beast." — p. 33
> 5. They viewed battle with the "... orbs of a jaded horse." — p. 37

Chapter Five

Writing the Paper

The time has finally come to sit down and write your paper. If you have carefully followed all the procedures outlined thus far, this will not be as formidable a task as it might seem. While doing your reading, you kept revising your preliminary outline, adding topics, deleting others, condensing some and expanding others—at the same time making corresponding changes in the topics on your note cards—so that now your preliminary outline is, for the most part, the outline of your paper. Working from your notes and taking into consideration your audience, point of view, tone, and purpose, you are ready to begin the first draft.

WORKING FROM NOTE CARDS

Since you have been constantly revising your outline while keeping your thesis statement in mind, your notes will reflect your outline. All that remains is to organize these cards into groups according to the topic headings and then organize the cards within these groups in the order you want to deal with them. It is here that the extra care and time devoted to taking neat note cards pays off. It will not be necessary to devote long hours to several readings of your notes, to revising notes, to circling and tagging items as you would have had to do had you taken them helter-skelter on long sheets of paper. The notes are organized and neat and all that remains is to organize them into the proper sequence. Then you only have to spread a group of cards before you to see at a glance the information that is available. Of course, you must realize there is no need to make use of all the notes you have taken. If you've done your job well, you will have more notes than are necessary. This is not only to be expected but is desirable.

THE FIRST DRAFT

Before beginning to write, you should clarify your primary objective so that everything in the paper is directed toward that end. This objective must either be stated or implied in the introduction, the length of which is determined by the total length of the paper; the longer the paper, the longer the introduction. A preface or formal introduction usually is not necessary in shorter papers—2,000 to 3,000 words—but is recommended in the longer ones, especially in theses. Here the reader will be informed of the purpose, tone, and attitude of the writer so that he will easily be able to follow the argument in the body.

The body of the paper, the development of the introduction is, of course, the most important and longest part. It is here that you present in an organized, coherent, unified, and forceful manner, all the material that you have spent countless hours gathering. However, be careful not to present a "cut-and-paste" project. You must do more than simply report facts gleaned from the reading or a compilation of other people's thinking. The value of a paper is not judged by the number of footnotes present or by the number of quotations used. If the paper is to have merit and stimulate the reader, then it must be written to reflect your careful consideration and understanding of your readings, your contemplation of what you have read, and your own thinking on the subjects, which all lead to a sound conclusion.

The length of the body of the paper determines the length of the conclusion. It may range from a paragraph in the short paper to a full chapter in the thesis. Whatever the length, it is not necessary to say "in conclusion." The ending should so logically sum up the material presented that there can be no doubt that this is the end. The ideal way to write the first draft is by using a word processor. Anyone who has ever used one knows that correcting, inserting, deleting, and moving text requires little effort and eliminates the need for time-consuming rewriting. It will also simplify the writing and placing of footnotes.

If you choose to write your first draft in longhand, then you should use wide-lined paper and a pen. You should write on alternate lines or on every third line, leaving ample room for revisions. You should also leave ample margins on both left and right, and number the pages consecutively. You should write clearly and legibly, paying attention to proper sentence structure, paragraphs, spelling, and grammar, but not to the point where it will interfere with your concentration on the content. Once you have utilized some information from your note cards, you should check off these items.

Regardless of how you prepare the first draft, you should first be sure you have certain essential references at your fingertips. Of paramount importance is a good recently revised dictionary. In addition, you will find Roget's *Thesaurus* and a good writer's handbook on grammar and usage of great value. When in doubt, do not hesitate to utilize these sources. You will find that if you pay attention to the mechanical and grammatical aspects of the first draft, you will be able to concentrate on the important element of style in your revision. The first draft should be complete, though unpolished. It is important to make a draft of the title page, introductory pages, table of contents, and bibliography for these too may need revision before the final paper is completed.

COHERENCE AND UNITY

In order for a piece of writing to be readily understood by a reader, it must be unified and coherent. That is to say, every item and every thought must be relevant to the primary thesis and all items must logically relate to each other.

The unity of a paper is maintained by carefully organizing your thoughts into paragraphs—each paragraph expressing a separate idea through a series of related sentences developing the idea that was expressed or implied in the topic sentence. You must be sure that each paragraph and each sentence in the paragraph is relevant to your major thesis. If you find that any idea does not aid in the development of the thesis, then that idea, regardless of how interesting it may be in its own right, does not belong in a unified paper.

Unity in a paper does not necessarily imply coherence. Coherence can be achieved in several ways, including:

- *The use of transitional words or phrases, such as on the other hand, in addition, nevertheless, and furthermore*
- *Repetition of key thoughts, words, or phrases*
- *Partial restatement of ideas; use of synonyms for key words*
- *Use of parallel grammatical structure*
- *Consistent use of the same point of view*
- *Logical organization of the information and arguments*

After you have asked yourself whether each thought and idea is relevant to the thesis statement and whether it adds something to what has already been said, you should ask one additional question: Does it logically follow that which precedes it and is it properly joined to the thought or idea that follows it? If the answer is yes, then the paper is coherent.

POINT OF VIEW

Point of view is the term generally used to indicate the point from which the paper is written. That is, first person or third person. In very formal papers, the first person singular "I" is not generally used. Instead, the writer referring to himself in the third person singular, e.g., "the author," "the researcher," "the writer" is. In less formal papers, the writer may sometimes make use of the first person plural, the editorial "we." However, usage leans more and more toward the less formal and stiff "I." Unless the student's instructor or adviser has some definite objection, the first person "I" is highly recommended.

SOME ASPECTS OF STYLE

This section makes no attempt to present a complete discussion of all aspects of style, nor does it pretend to be a grammar and usage text. For a reference source that will deal with all aspects of style, grammar, and correct usage, you should refer to a good grammar text. A freshman English handbook will serve this purpose. All that is intended here is to make you cognizant of some of the more troublesome areas.

Sentence structure

a. *Errors in structure:* Two of the most common errors in sentence structure, the run-on or comma splice and the fragment, must be avoided at all costs. To be sure, either one of these can be used stylistically, but you must exercise the greatest caution. When used correctly, the run-on and fragment are very effective, but if used incorrectly are very serious errors.

The run-on is primarily an error in punctuation. That is to say, two thoughts run together without proper punctuation separating these thoughts. The run-on sentence can be corrected by:

- *Placing a period at the end of the first thought and capitalizing the first word of the second thought*
- *Placing a semicolon between the two thoughts*
- *Using a comma and a coordinating conjunction (and, but, for, nor, or, yet, so) between the two thoughts*

The fragment is an incompletely stated thought whose incompletion may be due to the omission of the subject, the verb, or the complement. It may also be caused by using a verbal in place of a verb or by not completing a thought begun with a dependent clause. In any case, the fragment is corrected by supplying the missing part.

Other errors in structure include the dangling or misplaced modifier, awkward phrasing, and lack of parallelism. If you suspect that your sentence contains any one of these errors, then you should refer to your handbook for proper methods of correction.

b. *Subordination:* Subordination is the technique of placing the less important thought in a subordinate position. The dominant idea should always be expressed in the main clause. Subordinate clauses can be adverbial, adjectival, or substantive in function. In other words, these groups of words, containing a subject and verb, can function in the sentence in the same manner as an adverb, adjective, or noun. Subordinate thoughts that are not important enough to contain subject and verb should be expressed in phrases.

c. *Variety:* It is variety in sentence structure and sentence opening that avoids monotony, makes the paper more readable, and enables you to express yourself more effectively through the nuances in meaning reflected by the structure.

Basic structure of the sentence can be varied by compounding ideas or subordinating one idea to another. It can further be effected by using items in series; by using a series of short sentences; by effective use of involved, involuted sentence structure; by rearranging the normal subject-verb-complement pattern, and by varying sentence length.

Variations of sentence openings can be achieved by beginning a sentence with an adverbial clause, a prepositional phrase, a verbal (participle, gerund, infinitive) phrase, an expletive (a word such as *there*, which has no grammatical function in the sentence), a parenthetical expression (in fact, on the other hand), an adverb, an adjective, or a coordinate conjunction. Be cautioned that although any of the above will give you variety, they cannot be used interchangeably, for each variation will affect the meaning of the sentence.

Abbreviations

Abbreviations should not be used in thesis papers, with the exception of the names of well-known organizations (after the name has been written out once) and for certain instances in footnote and bibliographic entries.

Numbers

Generally, all numbers that consist of one or two words are written out. In addition, any number that is the first word in a sentence must also be written out. Numerals are to be used for:

- *Numbers consisting of more than two words*
- *Numbers used in tabulations*
- *Numbers used in statistical discussions*
- *Sums of money*
- *Numbers used in addresses and dates*
- *Numbers used to express time of day when used with A.M. and P.M., but not with o'clock*
- *Page numbers, volume numbers, and chapter and verse number*

Italics

Italicize an item by selecting the italic type style. In a typed manuscript, italics are indicated by underlining the item.

a. *Emphasis:* Italics may be used in lieu of quotation marks or capitalization to stress a word or phrase in the text. However, they must be used sparingly if they are to be effective. When you want to stress a word or phrase within a direct quotation, you may also use italics. But you then must state in brackets, not parentheses, that you have supplied the italics.

b. *Foreign terms:* Foreign terms that have not been anglicized must be italicized. Since there is disagreement, in some cases, as to which terms have been anglicized, you should use a recent edition of a good dictionary as your guide.

c. *Titles:* Titles of full-length books, newspapers, magazines, periodicals, and unpublished manuscripts are italicized. Titles of works that are part of a collection are placed within quotation marks.

d. *Italicized words in sources:* Words or phrases that appear in italics in the quoted source must also be italicized when quoted.

Contractions

Contracted forms should not be used. The only exception occurs when they appear in material that you wish to quote. In such instances, you should not use *sic*.

Punctuation

You should refer to a grammar handbook for all the rules for the proper use of punctuation marks. Here, however, are some rules that need special emphasis:

a. *Final punctuation:* Only one final punctuation mark is used. At no time will there be a double period, or a question mark followed by a period. The only exception would occur where the sentence ends with an abbreviation; then the period indicating the abbreviated form is followed by the question mark or the exclamation point, but never by another period.

b. *Punctuation preceding final quotation mark:* The comma and period always precede the final quotation mark. All other punctuation marks precede the final quotation mark when they are part of the quotation, and follow the mark when they are not.

c. *Parentheses and brackets in quotations:* Brackets and parentheses are not to be confused. Brackets are only to be used for the insertion of editorial comment within a quotation. Anything appearing within parentheses is part of the original quotation.

d. *Ellipse:* The omission of any part of a quotation is indicated by three spaced dots. When the omission occurs at the end of a sentence, a fourth dot representing the period is added.

Tense

For a detailed discussion of the function, form, and correct use of tense, mood, and voice, you should again consult your handbook. However, the following points are worthy of emphasis:

a. *Past tense:* Generally speaking, most papers are written in the past tense. Occasionally, however, you may want to make use of the historical present to give greater emphasis to his content. This form should be used sparingly.

b. *Present tense:* Aside from its use in the historical present, the present tense is also employed in critical comments (except biographical references where the subject is deceased) and in stating universal truths. There is a distinct difference, for instance, between saying "*Hamlet* was one of the greatest plays" and "*Hamlet* is one of the greatest plays."

c. *Consistency:* Although changes in tense are permissible, you must be careful not to shift the tense haphazardly in your paper. Unnecessary shifts in tense, aside from affecting clarity and style, will ruin the unity.

Reference of pronouns

Always exercise great care to ensure that when using a pronoun you have either stated or clearly implied a definite antecedent. Pronouns must agree with their antecedents in person, gender, and number. When using such indefinite pronouns as *anyone* or *someone*, the third person singular must be used. Some people object to using a masculine pronoun to refer to both a male and female and prefer using the cumbersome *he/she*. Unless the college style sheet requires such usage, it is better to change the antecedent to a plural noun and then use the appropriate third-person plural pronoun.

Paragraphing

Since clarity of meaning is, to a great extent, dependent upon the logical expression of units of thought, you must organize paragraphs effectively. You should be aware of basic paragraph organization—topic sentence, development, and concluding sentence—and of the various methods of paragraph development. You must also pay close attention to paragraph unity and coherence and to proper transition from one paragraph to the next. *

Vocabulary

Words convey meaning, and the broader your vocabulary base, the easier it will be to express your thoughts. You should be cautioned against a slavish dependence on the *Thesaurus*, searching out "big" words because you feel they will be impressive. Very often, you will find that the word that best expresses an idea is the simplest one.

Spelling

When in doubt, check a dictionary for the correct, preferred spelling, even if it means checking every word. The easiest way to check for spelling errors is with the word processor's spell-check program. This highlights all the misspelled words in the document, which should then be checked in a dictionary.

Wordiness

Student writers tend to be verbose in the presentation of their ideas. Number of words alone does not reflect understanding, nor does it reflect thoroughness in research or presentation of material. Always be concise. If you find that a paragraph can be condensed to one sentence or that the sentence can be condensed to a subordinate clause, the clause to a phrase, or the phrase to a word, or if the word can be eliminated altogether, make the reduction. Then, if you have a 3,000-word paper, they will be 3,000 meaningful words.

---

*For a more detailed discussion of paragraph organization and development, see Chapter Twelve, pp. 90-97.

PROOFREADING AND REVISION

After the first draft has been completed, it should be set aside for several days so you can approach it with a degree of objectivity. If you reread the paper immediately, then you will discover that you are not actually reading what you have written, but what you think you have written.

In proofreading a paper, you should consciously check for all errors in grammar, mechanics, structure, and style. Do not hesitate to rewrite whole portions of the paper if it is warranted. Always check for accuracy of quotations, proper documentation, and inadvertent plagiarism. Make sure you have presented your material and your argument forcefully and coherently. Check your facts against your notes. In short, the proofreading must take into account all aspects of content, structure, and style. Before you begin writing your final manuscript, there should not be the slightest doubt in your mind that this is one of the best pieces of research and writing you have done.

Chapter Six

The Format of the Thesis Paper

Once you have completed your first draft and have made all necessary revisions and corrections—which might necessitate the rewriting of the paper in either part or whole—you are ready to write the final paper (*see chapter 11*). It is at this point that the question of correct format arises. Although basic format varies very infrequently, you should be sure to check with your instructor or adviser for any special instructions or variation in the form.

Generally speaking, thesis papers consist of three parts:

1. Materials preceding the text

2. The text

3. References and appendices

The length of the content and the extensiveness of the research determine the length of any of these three parts. To be sure, in the short paper, materials preceding the text may consist of nothing more than the title page, and the references and appendixes will be limited to a listing of sources consulted in the preparation of the paper.

The following is the order in which the various items under each of the parts must be listed:

1. Materials preceding the text
   a. Title page (followed by a blank page)
   b. Preface, including acknowledgments
   c. Table of contents
   d. List of tables
   e. List of illustrations
2. The text
   a. Introduction
   b. Body of the paper
   c. Conclusion

3. References and appendices
   a. References consulted in the preparation of the paper
   b. Other sources pertinent to the topic
   c. Appendixes

Although items under 1 and 3 may be omitted, the above sequence must be followed.[1]

MATERIALS PRECEDING THE TEXT

Title page

The title page must contain the following information:

1. Title of the paper

2. Name of the writer

3. Name of the course for which the paper was written

4. Name of the college

5. Date the paper is due (Of course, some instructors may require additional information)

In those instances where the college or instructor does not specify a particular title-page format, the above information should be attractively placed on the sheet. The best practice to follow is to place the title of the paper centered on the page in either uppercase or upper-lowercase letters. If the title is too long to be centered on one line, then it should be written in inverted pyramid form without, however, splitting words or phrases. Titles should not be underlined or placed within quotation marks. Below the title, you should place your full name—first name then last name. In the lower left-hand corner, you should indicate the course for which the paper is being written. To the right of this, next to the right-hand margin, the name of the college and, below it, the due date.

Preface

The preface, sometimes referred to as the foreword, is a brief statement of the scope, aim, and general character of the research. It should not be confused with the introduction, which is an essential part of the text. The preface follows the blank sheet

---

[1]For samples, see Appendix Two, pp. 125-127.

after the title page and is headed PREFACE. In most short papers, a preface is unnecessary.

Table of contents

The table of contents is necessary only in those papers where the text has been divided into chapters. Here again, shorter papers will, in all probability, not require a table of contents. Where a table of contents is necessary, the heading TABLE OF CONTENTS should be centered on the sheet and typed in uppercase letters. Under the heading *Chapter*, at the left margin, chapter numbers are listed in large Roman numerals, aligned by the period following each numeral. Chapter headings are capitalized throughout. Page numbers are listed at the right margin in Arabic numerals under the heading *Page*.

Although subtitles do not have to be included in the table of contents, it is highly recommended that you include them. Subtitles enable the reader to see the basic outline of the work at a glance, and just as you found this a boon in the preparation of the paper, so will your reader. When the subtitles are listed, they are typed in upper-lowercase letters. The first letter of the first word and all nouns, pronouns, adjectives, adverbs, and verbs are capitalized. All headings and subtitles must correspond exactly with the headings as they appear in the body of the paper.

List of tables

Where several tables have been included in the text, you must prepare a list of tables, which follows the table of contents. The heading, LIST OF TABLES, should be centered on the sheet and typed in capitals. Under the heading *Table*, at the left, table numbers are listed in Arabic numerals; the corresponding page numbers are listed under *Page* at the right-hand margin. Next to the table number, the title of the table is typed in upper-lowercase letters. No list of tables is necessary where only one or two tables have been included in the text.

List of illustrations

The list of illustrations will be in the same form as the list of tables. The sheet will be headed LIST OF ILLUSTRATIONS, and the numbers of the illustrations, in Arabic numerals, will be listed at the left margin; the illustration title will be in upper-lowercase letters; and the page numbers will be in Arabic numerals at the right-hand margin. Here again, one or two illustrations in the text will not necessitate the inclusion of a list of illustrations.

THE TEXT

The text is, of course, the most important part of the paper. Here you present your facts and argument. The more logically, coherently, and effectively you can do this, the better your chance of enlightening the reader and, where it is part of the overall purpose, of convincing the reader. Therefore, it becomes imperative that you devote the major portion of your energy to a careful organization and presentation of findings.

Introduction

Whether the introduction is one paragraph or a separate chapter, it is the reader's first contact with your thoughts and writing style. If we are to assume that the reader is under no compulsion to read the paper, then the only criterion that will cause her to continue reading is sustained interest. If the introduction is dull, redundant, or confusing, the reader will simply put the text down. You must remember that there is absolutely nothing that will force a reader back to a paper once she has rejected it. The opening, therefore, must be vivid, interesting, and stimulating. It must capture the reader's attention.

The overall length of the paper will determine the length of the introduction. Shorter papers (2,000-3,000 words) need little more than a well-developed introductory paragraph. Longer papers may need chapter-length introductions.

Where the introduction is chapter-length, the page is headed CHAPTER I with the chapter title, INTRODUCTION, or some other descriptive title, below it. In those instances where the introduction is short but where the paper has been divided into chapters, you may simply want to head it INTRODUCTION without a chapter designation. In either case, however, the introduction is part of the text.

Body of the paper

The main part of the text focuses on the development of the aims stated or implied in the introduction. Careful organization, adequate substantiation, and proper documentation will aid in developing a logical and forceful argument. In longer papers where chapter divisions are a necessity, each main idea will begin on a new page headed with the chapter number and the title of the chapter in uppercase letters. In shorter papers, where there is no formal introduction, the argument should be developed without chapter divisions.

Conclusion

Just as the introduction is of prime importance in making the reader aware of what she will read, the conclusion is important in tying together all that she has read. Since the conclusion is the last part to be read, it, too, must be forceful, giving the reader the distinct impression of having gained something positive from the reading. The conclusion, as the introduction, may be either part of the paper or a separate chapter. In those instances where the conclusion is a separate chapter, it must be assigned a chapter number and a title, which may be CONCLUSION. However, a more descriptive title is preferred.

REFERENCES AND APPENDICES

References consulted

Following the text, you should list the sources you have consulted in the preparation of the paper. This bibliography should not contain all the sources that were examined but only those that had some definite bearing on the subject. If the bibliography is comparatively short, then all entries are arranged alphabetically, by author's last name, under the page heading BIBLIOGRAPHY or SOURCES CONSULTED. In longer bibliographies, sources are generally separated into two categories: texts and periodicals. If this practice is followed, then the subheadings *1. Texts* and *2. Periodicals* precede each grouping. The page heading remains as indicated above.

Other sources

On occasion, you may wish to supply a listing of works that the reader may consult for a more detailed and expanded study of the general topic. In such cases, you will list these works under the heading of SUPPLEMENTARY BIBLIOGRAPHY or ADDITIONAL SOURCES. These works will be listed in alphabetical order by author's last name.[1]

Appendices

Appendices serve the very useful function of permitting you to present additional information that is interesting and related to the topic, but not pertinent enough to be incorporated within the text. Included here may be such things as additional tables,

---

[1] For a more detailed discussion of bibliographies and for sample entries, see Chapter Nine, pp. 71-76.

sample questionnaires used in the study, copies of documents used but not generally available, and additional illustrative materials. If these items are comparatively short, then they may be listed under a single APPENDIX heading. If, on the other hand, each of these categories is extensive, then you should number the appendices and present each kind of material in a separate appendix. It is up to you to decide whether to place the appendices before or after the bibliography.

PAGINATION

Every page in a research paper except the blank sheet following the title page is assigned a number. From the title page up to, but not including, the first page of the research paper, small Roman numerals are used at the bottom of the page to designate the page number. These numerals are centered on the line and enclosed by dashes (e.g., -iv-). Although the title page is actually page -i-, it is not numbered. Therefore, the first page of the materials preceding the text will be numbered -ii-.

All other pages of the research paper, starting with the first page of the text, are numbered with Arabic numerals centered at the top of the page and enclosed by dashes. An exception in the placement of page numbers occurs for pages with chapter headings, including such headings as BIBLIOGRAPHY and APPENDIX. Here the page number is centered on the line at the bottom of the page. On a word processor, the format and placement of page numbers can be automatically configured. You can refer to your software's user manual.

TITLES AND SUBTITLES

Where the paper is divided into chapters, you may head each new chapter CHAPTER, followed by the appropriate number in large Roman numerals. This is centered on the line and below that is placed the chapter title in uppercase letters. You may prefer to eliminate the word *chapter* and place the Roman numeral immediately preceding the title.

Regardless of which method you use, each chapter must begin on a separate page with a concise, vivid chapter heading. Chapter headings must either clearly state or imply the contents of that which follows. Should the title be long, it must be divided and centered in an inverted pyramid. End punctuation other than the question and exclamation marks is not used.

The placement of subtitles depends on the number of subdivisions in any given chapter. If you are using only one rank of subdivision, then the subtitle is then placed at the margin, followed by a period and a dash, and is italicized. If there is to be a further subdivision, then the first subtitle is centered on the line and italicized, and the second subtitle is placed at the margin. All subtitles centered on the line are written in upper-lowercase; titles placed at the margin are written in lowercase except for the first letter of the first word, which is capitalized. All titles should be concise, pertinent, and descriptive.

For sure, there are possible variations in pagination, chapter headings, and subtitles. In the final analysis, you must be guided by your instructor or by the college style sheet. Where no specific instructions are given, you should follow the procedure outlined here.

Chapter Seven

Quotations

When taking notes, you may decide to copy certain information verbatim from your sources. Now, while writing your paper, you must determine which and how much of these quotations you will incorporate. The novice writer may well succumb to quoting too freely, feeling that she can never express the ideas as effectively as the writer of the source. This, however, would be unadvised, for nothing contributes as much to dull writing as a series of long quotations connected by brief bridging passages. Furthermore, lengthy quotations may cause the reader to forget whether he is reading an excerpt or the writer's own ideas. It is best to keep direct quotations as short as possible and to use them sparingly.

WHEN TO QUOTE

Although you must decide when to quote, taking into account the proposed quotation and the context in which it will be used, there are certain guidelines you can follow. If you find that any changes in the phrasing would alter the author's meaning or effect, then you should quote the passage. However, this decision is not simply based on your inability to state the idea as well stylistically; the paraphrase would have to be detrimental to the overall effect of the passage in order to warrant a direct quote. The passage should also be quoted where the changes in phrasing of the author's description of a procedure might cause misunderstanding.

In both instances, as well as in any other instance where you decide to quote, you must be guided by the principle that a careful paraphrase that does complete justice to the source is preferable to a lengthy quotation. Furthermore, you should avoid quotations that run several paragraphs. In many instances, there is not even a need to quote complete sentences. You can just as readily quote the pertinent part of the statement and incorporate it within your own sentence structure. To be sure, direct quotations tend to enhance the paper and to lend it greater validity, but only when they are used with discretion.

DIRECT PROSE QUOTATIONS

Short direct prose quotations—usually no longer than two sentences—should be included in the text enclosed in double quotation marks. When a quotation occurs within the passage being quoted, that portion is placed within single quotation marks.

> *Original:* The old man, shoving up the front of his tarpaulin and deliberately rubbing the long slant scar at the point where it entered the thin hair, laconically said, "Baby Budd, *Jemmy Legs*" (meaning the master-at-arms) "is down on you."

> *Quoted:* "The old man, shoving up the front of the tarpaulin and deliberately rubbing the long slant scar at the point where it entered the thin hair, laconically said, 'Baby Budd, *Jemmy Legs*' (meaning the master-at-arms) 'is down on you.'"

Note that in the above example, both single and double quotation marks are used, since there is dialogue within the quoted passage. However, if only the dialogue within the passage were quoted, only single quotation marks should be used:

> *Original:* "And that's because he's down upon you, Baby Budd."

> *Quoted:* 'And that's because he's down upon you, Baby Budd.'

When quotations are longer—two or more sentences and/or four or more typewritten lines—they should be set off from the text and indented both left and right. In double-spaced manuscripts, these longer quotations are single spaced and are not enclosed with quotation marks. It should be noted that the definition of "longer quotation" is somewhat arbitrary and may be modified. For emphasis, shorter quotations may also be set off from the text, but they should run at least two typewritten lines. If you are using a word processor, then you should set the quotation in smaller type.

> *Original:* Villains, whatever fate befell them in the obligatory last panel, were infinitely better equipped than those silly, hapless heroes. Not only comics, but life taught us that. Those of us raised in ghetto neighborhoods were being asked to believe that crime didn't pay? Tell that to the butcher! Nice guys finished last; landlords, first. Villains by their simple appointment to the role were miles ahead. It was not to be believed that any ordinary human could combat them. More was required. Someone with a call. When Superman at last appeared, he brought with him the deep satisfaction of all underground truths: our reaction was less, "How original!" than, "But, of course!"

> *Quoted:* Villains, whatever fate befell them in the obligatory last panel, were infinitely better equipped than those silly, hapless heroes. Not only comics, but life taught us that. Those of us raised in ghetto neighborhoods were being asked to believe that crime didn't pay? Tell that to the butcher! Nice guys finished last; landlords first. Villains by their simple appointment to the role were miles ahead. It was not to be believed that any ordinary human could

combat them. More was required. Someone with a call. When Superman at last appeared, he brought with him the deep satisfaction of all underground truths: our reaction was less, "How original!" than, "But, of course!"

Note that the quotation is an exact reproduction of the original. When a quotation appears within the passage, that quotation is placed within double quotation marks. Otherwise, no quotation marks are placed outside of the quoted passage.

Meticulous care must be taken to reproduce a quotation exactly. This means that it must be copied without any changes whatsoever. Every punctuation mark, every capitalization, every italicized word, even every spelling error, must be faithfully reproduced. However, to protect yourself, you must indicate that the error in the passage—whether it be a misspelling or an obviously ungrammatical sentence—is not your own by placing the Latin word *sic* (meaning *thus*) in brackets immediately following the error. The term *sic* must be italicized. However, the term should not be overused. Passages written in substandard English or in Spenserian English, for example, should not be strewn with *sic*s.

> *Original:* Television has become an important medium of communication in our modern society, and teachers would do well to recognize the valuable and important part this medium can play in the teaching program.
>
> *Quoted:* "Television has become an important medium of communication in our modern [*sic*] society, and teachers would do well to recognize the valuable and important part this medium can play in the teaching program."

When a passage runs two or more paragraphs, each paragraph is preceded by double quotation marks, but closing quotation marks are placed only at the end of the last paragraph. This is true only when the quotation is double-spaced. Setting off the passage from the text and single spacing is preferred.

POETRY QUOTATIONS

Quotations of verse that run two or more lines should be set off from the text, single-spaced, and centered on the line. No quotation marks should be used unless they appeared in the original. Here, you must exercise meticulous care to reproduce the material exactly.

When short poetic quotations are included within the text, they are enclosed in double quotation marks. In this case, however, the end of the poetic line is indicated by the use of the slash, e.g., "Stone walls do not a prison make, / Nor iron bars a cage." No slash is placed after the last line quoted. In setting off longer quotations from the text, the writer must also make certain that he follows the poet's indentations or visual arrangement of the lines. For example:

> If to be absent were to be
>   Away from thee;
>   Or that when I am gone,
>   You or I were alone,
>   Then, my Lucasta, might I crave
> Pity from blustering wind or swallowing wave.

ELLIPSES

Omissions in quotations are permitted when you feel that the portion is not necessary. However, great care must be exercised that the tone, meaning, or intent of the passage is not altered. The symbol for the ellipsis is three spaced periods (. . .). When an ellipsis occurs at the end of the passage, a fourth period—the end punctuation mark—is added. When quotation marks are used, the ellipsis is always enclosed within the quotation marks.

> *Original:* Humble and rustic life was generally chosen, because, in that condition, the essential passions of the heart find a better soil in which they can attain their maturity, are less under restraint, and speak a plainer and more emphatic language.
>
> *Quoted:* "Humble and rustic life was generally chosen, because, in that condition, the essential passions of the heart . . . speak a plainer and more emphatic language."

The ellipsis, of course, can occur at the beginning or end of the passage. Also there may be more than one ellipsis in any given passage. When you quote two or more paragraphs or two or more stanzas and wish to omit a complete paragraph or stanza, you can indicate this omission by a single line of spaced periods.

However, you must be cautioned about the careless use of ellipses. The omission of a single word can affect the meaning of an entire passage. Good scholarship and honesty demand that you check and recheck any passage in which an omission occurs to make certain that the meaning, tone, or intent has not been altered.

INTERPOLATION

There will be times when you find it necessary to insert an explanation or correction into the quotation. All such editorial comments must be placed within brackets, not parentheses.

The most common interpolations are the supplying of antecedents and the use of *sic* to indicate some error in the quotation. On occasion, however, you may want to stress a word or phrase in the quoted passage by italicizing it. You must then indicate that the italics are yours by stating "italics mine" or "emphasis added" within brackets following the emphasized word or phrase.

> *Supplying an antecedent:* "He [Henry Fleming] was not going to be badgered . . . like a kitten chased by boys . . . ."
>
> *Correction noted:* "William Shakesper [sic] probably wrote *Macbeth* in 1606 as a tribute to James II [I]."
>
> *Emphasis within quotation:* "Crafty men condemn studies, simple men admire them, and wise men use them; for *they teach not their own use* [italics mine]; but that there is a wisdom without them, and above them, won by observation."

INCORPORATING QUOTATIONS INTO YOUR WORDS

More often than not, you will want to quote only part of a passage and incorporate that within your own sentence structure. At such times, you must be certain that the quoted passage conforms to your own sentence structure and that pronoun reference and tense are consistent.

> *Original:* And there were iron laws of tradition and law on four sides. He was in a moving box.
>
> *Quoted:* Fleming instinctively looked for a way out but he was enclosed by the ". . . iron laws of tradition and law on four sides."

PUNCTUATING QUOTATIONS

The punctuation of quotations is in accord with two basic rules:

1. Periods and commas always precede the end quotation mark, even when the item consists of a single word or letter, e.g., "animal," "1st." There is no exception to this rule.

2. All other punctuation marks precede the end quotation mark when they are part of the quoted passage; when they are not, they follow the end quotation mark.

Examples:

"But why," he asked, "are you following this dangerous course?"

Does that mean we are condemning to death ". . . a fellow creature innocent before God . . ."?

Note that in the first example the quoted passage itself was an interrogative statement, but in the second example the quotation was not a question. Rather, it was the whole statement that was interrogative. In the case where both the quotation and the statement are questions, the question mark precedes the end quotation mark.

Another problem in punctuation is the mark preceding quotations. When the quotation is part of your sentence structure, the punctuation marks used are those that are demanded by the basic structure of the sentence. However, when the quotation is introduced by an explanatory or narrative tag—such as "Wordsworth in the *Preface* stated"—a comma follows the tag. When the quotation introduced is lengthy, which means that it would be single spaced and set off from the text, it is preceded by a colon.

FOOTNOTING QUOTATIONS

All direct quotations must be documented. The only possible exception is in the case of familiar quotations. However, it is wise to document even these. The footnote numeral should follow the final punctuation mark, or quotation mark, of the direct quotation when the MLA format is not being used.[1]

SECONDARY SOURCE QUOTATIONS

Ideally, you should not make any use of secondary sources. However, this is not always practical. In those instances where the primary source is not available or easily accessible, you will have to rely on the secondary source. It is imperative, though, that in your footnote you not only list the source you consulted but also the primary source. When the primary source is quoted within the quoted secondary text, the material from the primary source must be placed within single quotation marks.

---

[1]For footnoting procedures, see Chapter Eight, pp. 62-67.

ETHICS OF QUOTING

You must keep uppermost in your mind that using someone else's words or ideas without giving proper credit is literary theft for which you are legally and morally liable. Whether the lack of credit or improper documentation is due to carelessness or to basic dishonesty is immaterial. Hence, you must exercise the greatest caution that when quoting you are doing so accurately, retaining the author's words, punctuation (the omission of a comma might change the meaning), and tone. This is especially true when you make use of ellipses. In other words, you must check, recheck, and double-check every quotation you use against the source. Then, and only then, can you be reasonably certain of having done justice to the author.

Chapter Eight

Documenting Sources

Documenting sources is an important adjunct to the research paper. Here you can credit your sources and lend greater credence to your argument. Although you have some latitude in determining what to document, there are certain guidelines.

The two basic methods for documenting sources are the MLA and University of Chicago formats. The MLA style incorporates references to the sources parenthetically within the text. Since footnotes are not used, the reader is not interrupted. Although MLA style is generally preferred, you should also be familiar with the University of Chicago format.

When using the University of Chicago format, you are urged to write your footnotes during the preparation of your first draft. In this way, you will be able to determine the need for additional data that might have to be incorporated in the note. Also, it will allow you to proofread the notes and discover any errors in content or form so that you can make any necessary corrections.

PURPOSE OF DOCUMENTING SOURCES

Footnotes may be classified according to two types: reference and content. Reference notes give the publication facts of sources cited or make references to other parts of the paper. Content footnotes allow you to give additional information that you feel is of interest to the reader yet is not vital enough to be incorporated into the text.

REFERENCE NOTES

Facts used in a research paper that are commonly known are public property and may be used without any acknowledgment; but any other fact or any idea that is not public property must be credited to the original author. The following items must be documented:

1. Direct quotations
2. Statements that are paraphrased

3. All statements that are not generally accepted as true

4. Any opinion or idea that did not originate from the writer

Prior knowledge on your part does not affect footnoting. That is to say that even if you never knew a certain fact, and have just learned it, you would not need to footnote it if it is common knowledge.

In addition to the above-mandated footnotes, reference notes also include the "see-also" note. Here you may wish to call the reader's attention to additional information either in some other text or in some other part of your paper.

CONTENT NOTES

Content footnotes are very similar to appendices. Here you have the opportunity to expand, amplify, or comment on the information presented in the text. You may also present interesting sidelights on the topic under discussion, quote additional sources, or expand the discussion with additional details. Regardless of what you incorporate here, you are restricted by the fact that the content note must be relevant, albeit tangential, to the topic under discussion in the text. In writing the content note, you must be guided by good English. You must adhere to proper sentence structure, paragraphing, and coherence. If you make reference to another source, you must give pertinent publication facts.

MLA STYLE

Before using this style for documenting sources, you must have a complete bibliography so that its information matches the parenthetical references. *(See chapter 9 for bibliographic entries.)* You then need to give only enough information for the reader to readily locate the source. This information would include the author's name, if not mentioned already in the passage, and the page number(s) of the source.

Author's name in bibliography but not in passage

If there is only one work by the author cited, you only need to list the author's last name (and the first initial if there is more than one author with the same last name). If there are two or more works by the same author, you must add the title, or a shortened version, after the author's name. If there are two or three authors, you must list the last name of each. If there are more than three authors, you must list the last name of the first author followed either by *et al.* or "and others." When there is no author listed, you must give the title or a shortened version thereof. Here are some examples:

One author: The "Bright Star" sonnet was originally written to Mrs. Isabella Jones (Daiches 338).

Two or more works by the same author: "Now, with the newborn question in his mind, he was compelled to sink back into his old place as part of a blue demonstration" (Crane, *Red Badge* 12).

Two or three authors: Ellen Terry gave the crushing reply to all literary detective work when she argued that, by the same criteria, Shakespeare must have been a woman (Wellek and Warren 67).

No author listed: At night he went to see how the Danes had acted after the beer banquet ("Beowulf" 5).

When the passage that is documented contains more than one sentence, the source citation follows the end punctuation mark. If, however, the passage being documented is part of a sentence, then the citation follows that part.

Author's name in passage

When the author's name has been mentioned in the passage, you only need to give the page number(s):

Ellen Terry, according to Wellek and Warren, gave the crushing reply to all literary detective work when she argued that, by the same criteria, Shakespeare must have been a woman (67).

Documenting quotations

For short quotations the source information follows the end quotation mark but precedes the period. For longer quotations, two or more sentences and/or four or more typed lines set off from the text, the source information follows the end punctuation of the quoted passage.

Secondary source citations

If the primary source is not available, then it may be necessary to use the secondary source. In that case, *qtd. in* (quoted in), if it is a direct quotation, or *ctd. in* (cited in), if it is not, precedes the secondary source citation. It is advisable to document the primary source in a content footnote. For example:

As John F. Kennedy so eloquently stated in his Inaugural Address, '. . . ask not what America can do for you, but what together we can do for the freedom of man' (qtd. in Quinn and Dolan 62).

You should give sufficient information to enable the reader to locate a passage easily. This may necessitate incorporating chapter, stanza, lines, and even primary source data within the parentheses.[1]

UNIVERSITY OF CHICAGO STYLE

Although the MLA style is relatively new and much simpler to use, it is important to familiarize yourself with the University of Chicago format since it has been in use for a long time, and especially if your instructor or university mandates it. You will also find it helpful to understand such entries as *ibid., op. cit., loc. cit.,* and *passim.*

PLACING AND NUMBERING FOOTNOTES

Footnotes may be placed in any one of three places: at the bottom of the page, at the end of the chapter, or at the end of the paper, in which case they are called endnotes. Placement at the bottom of the page is preferred. Footnotes are there for the convenience of the reader. Everyone has been annoyed by having to turn to the end of the text for a footnote only to discover that it was a source citation. When footnotes appear at the bottom of the page, the reader need only glance down to see whether the note is of interest to her.

All footnote references—with the exception of those in mathematical texts where a footnote number may be mistaken for an exponent—use Arabic numerals. Although notes may be renumbered on each page, they generally are numbered consecutively throughout each chapter. Where the paper is not divided into chapters, footnotes should be numbered consecutively throughout. The footnote number is placed following the statement—and the punctuation mark—to which the note refers. It is raised one-half space (superscript) and is not followed by a period or enclosed in dashes or parentheses, nor is it circled.

A correspondingly numbered note at the bottom of the page must represent every footnote number in the text. These footnotes are separated from the text by a double-space and a solid line from the left-hand margin and as long as the longest line on that page. Footnote entries are single-spaced with a double-space between them.

---

[1] For a more detailed discussion of the MLA style, see Joseph Gibaldi, *MLA Handbook for Writers of Research Papers*, 4th ed. (New York: The Modern Language Association of America, 1995).

Where footnote numbers might be confused with mathematical figures, you must use a series of symbols, such as the asterisk, cross, or double cross, which must be reused on every page where information is to be documented.

FIRST MENTION OF A REFERENCE

The first time a work is cited, it must include all the information necessary for easy location of the work. The footnote should include the author's full name, the title of the work, the facts of the publication, and the volume and page numbers. This information should be arranged as follows:

1. Author's first name, middle initial, and last name, followed by a comma

2. Title of the book, underlined

3. Place and date of publication, separated by a comma and enclosed in parentheses, followed by a comma

4. Volume number, in large Roman numerals, followed by a comma

5. Page number, followed by a period

This data is then placed at the bottom of the page, immediately below the solid horizontal line. The footnote numeral is indented and raised, and the footnote is single-spaced. Second and successive lines of the entry are brought to the left margin.

PUNCTUATING FOOTNOTES

The title of any work published separately must be italicized. Titles of works incorporated within a text are enclosed in quotation marks. Names of the books of the Bible, titles of ancient manuscripts, and legislative acts and bills are never italicized or placed within quotation marks.

All words in a title with the exception of prepositions, articles, and conjunctions are capitalized. The only exception occurs in cases like e e cummings' poetry, where the poet wrote the title in all lowercase letters. However, you may capitalize such titles. A period is placed at the end of all footnote entries.

When a book title includes the title of a selection in the book, the selection title is placed within quotation marks and the entire title is italicized. Conversely, when the title of an article, for example, includes the title of a book, the entire title is placed within quotation marks and the title of the book is italicized, such as "The Motif of the Wise Old Man in *Billy Budd*."

PUBLICATION FACTS

The essential publication facts that should be included in the footnote entry are the place and date of publication. Inclusion of the publishing company is superfluous, since this fact can be found in the bibliography. Where more than one place of publication is listed in the source book, the first one—or the place geographically nearest—is to be used. The date of publication is the date of the first printing. In the case of a revised edition, the date of that edition should be listed.

The publication facts should have been indicated on your bibliography cards. If the information was inadvertently omitted, you will then have to get the source and check the title and copyright pages for this information.

FOOTNOTE ENTRIES FOR FIRST REFERENCE TO A SOURCE

Book—one author
[1]Chaim Potok, *My Name Is Asher Lev* (New York, 1996), pp. 6-7.

Book—one author; numbered or revised edition
[2]Kimball Wiles, *Supervision for Better Schools,* 5th ed. (Englewood Cliffs, N.J., 1982), p. 156.

[*Note:* Since the place of publication given here is not generally known, the state must be indicated as well.]

Book—one author; more than one volume
[3]Vernon Louis Parrington, *Main Currents in American Thought* (Norman, OK, 1987), vol. II, pp. 112-113.

[*Note:* Since this reference contains both a volume and a page number, it is permissible to omit "vol." and "pp." This information would be designated as "II. 112-113." You should determine the method you prefer and then use it consistently throughout her paper. Also note the notation "c. 1930." The "c." designates *copyright,* and the entry is an indication that no publication date was available. If no date could have been found, then "n.d." (no date) would follow the place of publication.]

Book—two authors
[4]Ernest L. Boyer and Paul Boyer, *Smart Parents Guide to College* (Princeton, 1996), p. xi.

[*Note:* Where two or more authors are given, authors' names are not arranged alphabetically but in the order in which they appear on the title page. Also note that the page number refers to materials preceding the text.]

Book—more than three authors
[5]Lynda M. Applegate et al., *Corporate Information Strategy and Management: Text and Cases* (New York, 2002), p. 142.

[*Note:* In lieu of "*et al.*" the anglicized form "and others" may be used. Here again you should determine which form you prefer and use that form consistently throughout her paper.]

Book—no author given
[6]*The Lottery* (London, [1732]), pp. 9-10.

[*Note:* The brackets enclosing the publication date indicate that the date had been omitted from the title page and was located in the card catalog or some other reference work.]

Book—editor of a collection
[7]Joan Sherman, ed., *African-American Poetry of the Nineteenth Century* (Champaign, IL, 1992), p. 19.

[*Note:* The abbreviation "ed." or "eds." may be placed within parentheses. If this is done, the comma following the editor's name is omitted. The above entry should be used only when reference is made to the book as a whole and not to any selections within the book. *See sample footnotes 11 and 12.*]

Book—author and editor
[8]Stephen Crane, *The Red Badge of Courage,* ed. Richard Chase (Boston, c. 1960), pp. 21-22.

Book—translated into English
[9]Gustave Flaubert, *Madame Bovary,* trans. Gerard Hopkins (New York, 1959), pp. 215-216.

Book—no author or editor; translated
[10]*The Anglo-Saxon Chronicle.,* trans. G. N. Garmonsway (London, 1953), p. 131.

Book—article or essay by one of several contributors
[11]Paul Goodman, "Growing Up Absurd—'Human Nature' and the Organized System," *The Sense of the 60's,* eds. Edward Quinn and Paul J. Dolan (New York, 1968), pp. 9-10.

Article or essay—author given
[12]Terry Southern, "The Rolling Stones' U.S. Tour: Riding the Lapping Tongue," *Saturday Review,* 55:25, August 12, 1972.

[*Note:* In the entry "55:25," the number preceding the colon is the volume number, and the number following the colon is the page number. An alternate form is given below.]

Article or essay—no author given
[13]"South Viet Nam: Campaign of Brutality," *Time,* 100: 17-18, August 21, 1972..

Article or essay—initials of author given; full name supplied
[14]S[ebastian] H. G[unner], "Heresy in Education," *Journal of Educational Discourse,* 15:26-27, September, 1958.

Article or essay—alternate entry
[15]Terry Southern, "The Rolling Stones' U.S. Tour: Riding the Lapping Tongue," *Saturday Review,* LV (August 12, 1972) p 25.

Articles—encyclopedias, dictionaries, etc.
[16]"Drama—Stories on the Stage," *Compton's Pictured Encyclopedia* (1967), IV, 169.

[*Note:* If the above were a numbered or revised edition, the edition number would precede the year, such as (4th ed., 1967)

Newspaper
[17]*New York Times*, February 19, 2003, Sec. 4, p. 3.

Newspaper—title and author given
[20]Monte Hayes, "Trial Begins for Peru's Former Spy Chief," *The Washington Post*, February 19, 2003, p. A18.

[*Note:* When the title of the newspaper does not include the place of publication, it should be included within parentheses following the title.]

Newspaper—title given; no author
[21]"Bolivian Cabinet Resigns, Clearing Way for Shuffling of Posts" *The New York Times*, February 19, 2003, p. 3.

[*Note:* Whenever possible, the author and title of the article are given.]

Unpublished materials
[22]Harry Teitelbaum, "A Study of Leisure-time Reading Habits of Second Year High School Students" (Unpublished Brooklyn College Master's Thesis, 1953), pp. 30-32.

Biblical reference
[23]Matt. 2: 5-8.

[*Note:* The number preceding the colon refers to the chapter; the numbers following, the verses.]

Bulletin—institution or organization as author
[24]State University of New York at Stony Brook, 1991-92 *Graduate Bulletin* (Stony Brook, 1991), pp. 49-50.

Lecture
[25]John Sebastian, Lecture: "Naturalism in *The Red Badge of Courage,*" Community Literary Discussion Group, September 23, 1964.

Secondary source citation
[27]John Jones, *Famous Authors and Their Works* (New York, 1945), p. 25, citing Nathaniel Hawthorne, *The Scarlet Letter* (Boston, 1850), pp. 4-5.

Secondary source citation or quotation—alternate
[28]Nathaniel Hawthorne, *The Scarlet Letter* (Boston, 1850), pp. 4-5, cited by John Jones, *Famous Authors and Their Works* (New York, 1945), p. 25.

[*Note:* Either of these two forms is acceptable, but you should strive to be consistent in the form used within the paper.]

SECOND OR LATER MENTION OF A REFERENCE

After the first complete mention of a reference, later references to the source are made in shortened forms. This is true only when footnotes are numbered consecutively. Shortened forms may not be used for references cited in previous chapters; they must again be cited in full.

When references to the same work follow each other without any intervening reference, even though they are separated by several pages, the abbreviation *ibid.* (for the Latin *ibidem,* "in the same place") is used to repeat the preceding reference. Any changes in volume and/or page number(s) must be indicated following *ibid.* However, if the reference is to the same volume and page number as the preceding reference, then nothing follows *ibid. Ibid.* may not be used to repeat part of a preceding reference.

Examples:

[1] J. N. Hook, *The Teaching of High School English,* 5th ed., (New York, 1982), pp. 176-177.

[*Note:* The first and therefore complete reference to the work.]

[2] *Ibid.*

[*Note:* Since there are no intervening references, the second mention of the work requires only *ibid.* Note that since *ibid.* is never preceded by any other word, it is always capitalized. Also since footnote 2 refers to pp. 176-177, no page numbers need be indicated.]

[3] *Ibid.,* p. 39.

[*Note:* Since there have been no intervening references, *ibid.* is still correct; this time it refers to a different page. As long as there are no intervening references, *ibid.* may continue to be used.]

Use of *Op. Cit.*

Reference to a work that has already been cited in full form, but not in the reference immediately preceding, should include the author's last name (but not her first name or initials unless two authors by the same last name have already been mentioned in the paper), and the abbreviation *op. cit.* (for the Latin *opere citato,* "in the work cited"). In most of these entries, *op. cit.* is followed by the page designation.

Examples:

[1] Van Wyck Brooks, *The Confident Years: 1885-1915* (New York, 1955), p. 87.

[2] Frederick J. Hoffman, *The Twenties* (New York, 1965), pp. 189-190.

[3] Brooks, *op. cit.,* p. 81.

[*Note:* Since there was an intervening reference, *op. cit.* must be used and the new page designated.]

Use of *Loc. Cit.*

Loc. cit. (for the Latin *loco citato,* "in the place cited") is used in lieu of *ibid.* when the reference is not only to the work immediately preceding but also refers to the same page. *Loc. cit.* is also used in lieu of *op. cit.* when reference is made to a work previously cited and to the same page in that work. Hence, *loc. cit.* is never followed by volume and/or page numbers. When it takes the place of *ibid., loc. cit.* is capitalized.

Examples of Footnote Entries Using *Ibid., Op. Cit.,* and *Loc. Cit.*

[1]Jacqueline Sweeney, *Teaching Poetry* (New York, 1995), p. 93.

[2]J. N. Hook, *The Teaching of High School English*, 5th ed. (New York, 1982), pp. 66-67.

[3]*Ibid.,* pp. 138-139.

[*Note:* Refers to work by J. N. Hook. If the reference had been to the same pages, then *loc. cit.* would have been used.]

[4]Sweeney, *loc. cit.*

[*Note: Loc. cit.* is used since the note refers to p. 93.]

[5]*Ibid.,* pp. 77-79.

[*Note:* Reference is made to the work by Sweeney.]

[6]*Ibid.,* p. 20.

[*Note:* Reference is again made to Sweeney.]

[7]Benjamin A. Heydrick, *How To Study Literature* (New York, 1973) p. v.

[8]*Loc. cit.*

[*Note:* Reference is made to the note immediately preceding. Since the reference is to the same passage, *loc. cit.* is used instead of *ibid.* Note that since no word precedes the entry, *loc. cit.* has been capitalized.]

[9]Matthew Sweeney, *Writing Poetry and Getting Published* (Lincolnwood, IL, 1997), pp. 101-110.

[10]Hook, *op. cit.,* p. 79.

[11]Jacqueline Sweeney, *loc. cit.*

[*Note:* Since two works have been listed by authors with the same last name, the first name of the author must be given. *Loc. cit.* refers to footnote 6, the last reference made to that work.]

[12]*Ibid.,* pp. 29-30.

[*Note:* Refers to footnote immediately preceding.]

[13]Mario Pei, *The Story of English* (New York, 1952), p. 56.

[14]Matthew Sweeney, *op. cit.,* p. 5.

[15]Mario Pei, *Invitation to Linguistics: A Basic Introduction to the Science of Language* (Garden City, N.Y., 1965), pp. 48-49.

[16]Hook, *loc. cit.*

[17]Pei, *The Story of English*, p. 10.

[*Note:* Since two works have been listed by the same author, reference to either work must include the author's last name and title of the work being cited.]

QUICK TIPS TO REMEMBER

1. Footnote entries should be written when writing the first draft.

2. All entries should be checked for accuracy of information and form.

3. *Ibid., loc. cit.,* and *op. cit.* must be italicized.

4. All footnote entries are single-spaced. There is a double-space between all entries.

5. All entries are followed by a period.

6. The same bottom margin must be maintained on all pages, regardless of the number of footnotes.

7. Entries should be numbered consecutively except where the paper is divided into chapters. In that case, the first footnote entry in a chapter is "1."

8. Footnotes should be placed at the bottom of the page. Most word processing programs can automatically number the notes consecutively and place them at the bottom of the appropriate pages.[2]

9. Content notes must be written in clear, concise English. When the note is long, it should be incorporated into an appendix.

Always remember that the scholarship of your article will be judged by your documentation. The ability to refer to authorities and to substantiate your research is what lends credence to your argument.

---

[2] For more information on footnoting, see Kate L. Turabian, *A Manual for Writers of Term Papers, Theses, and Dissertations* (6th ed.: Chicago: The University of Chicago Press, 1996).

Chapter Nine

The Bibliography

The bibliography is part of the last section of the paper and follows the text. If there are appendices as well, the bibliography may precede or follow them. With the exception of very short research papers where a bibliography may be omitted (in that case, footnote entries must include the name of the publisher, following the place of publication), a formal bibliography is necessary. The bibliography may be limited to only those works that you found significantly relevant or include all works that were consulted in the preparation of the paper and that had any bearing whatsoever on the topic. In addition, you may wish to supply a listing of works that the reader may consult for a more detailed and expanded study of the general topic. Such a listing of additional sources, however, should be listed under a separate heading.

BIBLIOGRAPHICAL ORDER

The length of the bibliography will determine the basic classifications. In a comparatively short bibliography, all works will be listed under a single heading. In longer ones, where you consulted a number of works of many different kinds, you may choose to list these titles under separate subheadings, e.g., texts and periodicals. Conceivably, there may be even more subdivisions, e.g., public documents interviews, speeches, and reports.

Bibliographical entries are arranged alphabetically by author's last name. Where no author is listed, the work is listed by the first word of the title exclusive of any article (*a, an, the*), and the article is listed following the title, e.g., "Effects of the War, The." Works with no authors listed should not be listed under "Anonymous."

For all intents and purposes, your bibliography has already been arranged if you have followed the directions for the preparation of your working bibliography, and checked all his information against the books themselves. All that is necessary is for you to remove those cards that were irrelevant and, if necessary, arrange your sources according to type. After this, all that remains is transcribing the information from the cards.

SPACING

All bibliographical entries are single-spaced with double spaces between entries. The author's last name begins at the margin, and where the entry contains more than one line, successive lines are indented. The same indentation should be observed for all entries.

CONTENTS OF BIBLIOGRAPHICAL ENTRIES

Bibliographical entries contain these facts arranged as follows:

1. The author's last name, followed by a comma; the first name and middle initial, followed by a period.

2. The title of the work, followed by a period. Titles of full-length works are italicized (underlined); titles of works in collections are enclosed in double quotation marks. All words with the exception of articles, prepositions, and conjunctions—unless it is the first word in the title—are capitalized.

3. The edition number, followed by a period.

4. The name of the translator, compiler, or editor—where pertinent—followed by a period.

5. The place of publication, followed by a colon. If the city is not well known, the state should also appear, e.g., Garden City, New York. When more than one place of publication is given in the book, generally the first one is used.

6. The name of the publisher, followed by a comma.

7. The year of publication, followed by a period. If the date of publication does not appear on the title page but has been located elsewhere, it should be enclosed within brackets. If it cannot be located, then the approximate copyright date is given with the notation *c.* (circa) preceding it, e.g., *c.* 1956. Where neither date of publication nor copyright date is available, the notation *n.d.* (no date) is listed.

8. The number of pages in the work or the page numbers that contain relevant information, followed by a period. This entry is optional.

Compare the following bibliographical entries with the comparable footnote entries in the preceding chapter.

1. Book—one author
Potok, Chaim. *My Name Is Asher Lev*. New York: Ballantine Books, 1996.

2. Book—one author; numbered or revised edition
Lovell, John T. *Supervision for Better Schools,* 5th ed. Englewood Cliffs, New Jersey: Prentice-Hall, 1982.

3. Book—one author; more than one volume
Parrington, Vernon Louis. *Main Currents in American Thought*. Norman, Oklahoma: University of Oklahoma Press, 1987. 3 vols.

4. Book—one author; only one volume used
Parrington, Vernon Louis. *Main Currents in American Thought*. Norman, Oklahoma: University of Oklahoma Press, 1987. Vol. II.

5. Book—two authors
Boyer, Ernest L. and Boyer, Paul. *Smart Parents Guide to College*. Princeton, New Jersey: Peterson's, 1996.

[*Note:* When more than one author is listed, only the name of the first author is inverted; all other names are given in the first name-last name order.]

6. Book—more than three authors
Applegate, Lynda M. et al. *Corporate Information Strategy and Management: Text and Cases*. New York: McGraw-Hill/Irwin, 2002.

[*Note:* The words "and others" may be substituted for "*et al.*" However, the writer must use the same form as he did in the footnote entries.]

7. Book—no author given
Lottery, The. London: J. Watts, (1732).

[*Note:* The article is listed following the title for ease of alphabetization.]

8. Book—editor of a collection
Sherman, Joan R., ed. *African-American Poetry of the Nineteenth Century*. Champaign, Illinois: University of Illinois Press, 1992.

[*Note:* If "ed." was placed within parentheses in the footnote entries, it should be done here as well.]

9. Book—author and editor
Crane, Stephen. *The Red Badge of Courage*. Ed. Richard Chase. Boston: Houghton Mifflin Company, C. 1960.

10. Book—translated into English

Flaubert, Gustave. *Madame Bovary*. Trans. Gerard Hopkins. New York: Dell Publishing Company, Inc., 1959.

11. Book—no author or editor; translated

Anglo-Saxon Chronicle, The. Trans G. N. Garmonsway. London: J. M. Dent and Sons, Ltd., 1953.

12. Book—article or essay by one of several contributors

Goodman, Paul. "Growing Up Absurd—'Human Nature' and the Organized System," *The Sense of the 60's*. Eds. Edward Quinn and Paul J. Dolan. New York: Macmillan, 1968. Pp. 3-13.

15. Article or essay—author given

Southern, Terry. "The Rolling Stones' U.S. Tour: Riding the Lapping Tongue," *Saturday Review,* 55:25-30.August 12, 1972.

16. Article or essay—no author given

"South Viet Nam: Campaign of Brutality," *Time,* 100:17-18. August 21, 1972.

18. Article or essay—initials of author given; full name supplied

G[unner], S[ebastian] H. "Heresy in Education," *Journal of Educational Discourse,* 15:20-31. September, 1958.

19. Article or essay—alternate entry

Southern, Terry. "The Rolling Stones' U.S. Tour: Riding the Lapping Tongue," *Saturday Review,* Lv (August 12, 1972), 25-30.

[*Note:* The writer is to use whichever form he used in the footnote entries.]

20. Articles—encyclopedias, dictionaries, etc.

"Drama—Stories on the Stage," *Compton's Pictured Encyclopedia*. (1967), IV, 169-192.

21. Newspaper

New York Times, February 19, 2003, Sec. 4, p. 3.

22. Newspaper—title and author given

Hayes, Monte. "Trial Begins for Peru's Former Spy Chief," *The Washington Post*, February 19, 2003, p. 5.

[Note: When the title of the newspaper does not include the place of publication, it should be included within parentheses following the title.]

23. Newspaper—title given; no author
   "Bolivian Cabinet Resigns, Clearing Way for Shuffling of Posts," *The New York Times*, February 19, 2003, p. 3.

24. Unpublished materials
   Teitelbaum, Harry. "A Study of Leisure-time Reading Habits of Second Year High School Students. Unpublished Master's Thesis. Brooklyn, New York: Brooklyn College, 1953.

25. Bulletin—institution or organization as author
   State University of New York at Stony Brook. *1991-92 Graduate Bulletin*. Stony Brook, New York: University Press, 1991.

26. Lecture
   Sebastian, John. Lecture: "Naturalism in *The Red Badge of Courage*." Community Lecture Discussion Group, September 23, 1972.

ANNOTATION

Although completely optional, you may wish to annotate your bibliography for the convenience of the reader. When this is done, the annotation should be single-spaced and begin on the line following the bibliographical entry.

SAMPLE BIBLIOGRAPHY

The following is a sample of a bibliography at the end of a short paper. Note that the articles and periodicals are not separated from the rest of the entries. Also note that the entries are not numbered.

BIBLIOGRAPHY

Brown, Jared. *The Theatre in America During the Revolution*. New York: Cambridge University Press, 1995.

Chinoy, Helen K., and Linda Walsh Jenkins. *Women in American Theater*. New York: Theatre Communications Group, 1986.

Estavan, Lawrence. *Pioneer Families of the American Theatre*. San Bernardino, California: The Borgo Press, 1994.

McNamara, Brooks. *Plays from the Contemporary American Theatre*. New York: Mentor Books, 1996.

Mordden, Ethan. *The American Theatre*. New York: Oxford University Press, 1981.

Chapter Ten

Tables, Graphs, Illustrations

The purpose of tables, graphs, and illustrations is to aid in the discussion and explanation of information in the text. Hence, all illustrative materials must have a definite function and cannot just serve as window dressing. Wherever these materials seem superfluous, they should be omitted or, if you feel they have some limited merit, be included in the appendix. Regardless of where they are placed, they must be clear and understandable.

PLACEMENT

Wherever possible, illustrative materials should immediately follow their first mention in the text. However, if the insertion of the material at that point would necessitate continuing it onto the next page, you may continue with the text and place the illustrative materials on the following page.

TABLES

Tables are an important adjunct in any paper that is based on collected data of a statistical nature. Whenever figures are presented to the reader, they should be tabulated for easy reference. The inclusion of a long list of figures with the text will only serve to confuse the reader. However, it must again be stressed that tables cannot be included solely for their own sake. They must serve a definite purpose of reinforcing or clarifying the text.

Numbering tables

All tables, including those in the appendix, are numbered consecutively with Arabic numerals. The table number follows the word "TABLE" typed in uppercase letters and centered above the caption. Pages containing tables are numbered in the usual manner with the page number in Arabic numerals centered at the top of the page and enclosed with dashes.

Captions

Every table must have a caption—a concise statement describing its contents—placed above the table. The caption, typed in uppercase letters, is centered two lines below the table number. If the caption runs to two or more lines, then it is written in inverted pyramid form. No period follows the caption. A double unbroken line is drawn the width of the table two spaces below the caption.

Each column in the table must have an appropriate and descriptive heading; because of space limitation, the heading must be concise. When the column caption consists of more than one word and the column width does not permit it to be written on a single line, the caption is arranged so that it is pleasing to the eye and its meaning clear. Captions follow the rules for capitalization in titles.

Table layout

Neatness and ease of comprehension are the guiding principles in laying out tables. However, the following rules should be adhered to:

1. A double unbroken line is placed at the top of the table, two spaces below the caption.

2. A single horizontal line is placed at the bottom of the table.

3. No vertical rules are placed at either end of the table.

4. Columns are separated with vertical rules.

5. Items within the table may be single-spaced or double-spaced.

6. Two-column tables contain no vertical rules.

7. Abbreviations in column captions may be used, but if they are not standard abbreviations, they must be explained in a "key" at the bottom of the table.

8. All figures are aligned by the decimal points.

Footnotes

If it is necessary to include footnotes within the table, then they are placed below the bottom horizontal rule, and not at the foot of the page with other textual notes. To avoid confusion, lowercase letters, instead of Arabic numerals, are used to designate footnotes. If none of the tables has more than one footnote, then an asterisk may be used, but asterisks and letters may not be used interchangeably. Footnotes are single-spaced with a double-space between entries.

Long tables

Continue tables that run more than one page on the following page with the heading "TABLE—*Continued*" centered above the double unbroken line of the table. It is not necessary to repeat the table caption. If at all possible, however, tables should not be split between pages. When a table contains too many items for it to be listed vertically, it may be arranged horizontally on a separate page. The page number, however, should appear in the usual position.

Sample tables:

TABLE 1

MAGAZINES LISTED AS FIRST CHOICE

Name of Magazine	No.	%
Life	187	25.4
Sports magazines	89	12.1
Mechanical magazines	40	5.4
Science magazines	28	3.8
No choice indicated	331	45.0

TABLE 2

TYPES OF BOOKS PREFERRED BY HIGH SCHOOL STUDENTS (FIRST THREE CHOICES)

	Type of Book	No.	%
	First Choice		
Boys	Sports	174	23.7
Girls	Novels	219	50.6
Both	Novels	292	25.0
	Second Choice		
Boys	War Stories	113	15.4
Girls	Mystery	126	29.1
Both	Mystery	197	16.9
	Third Choice		
Boys	War Stories	99	13.5
Girls	Comics	73	16.9
Both	Comics	147	12.6

TABLE 3

DEGREE TO WHICH STUDENTS ARE FOND OF READING

Reading	Boys		Girls		Both	
Fondness	No.	%	No.	%	No.	%
Very much	111	15.1	98	22.6	209	17.9
Quite a lot	217	29.5	164	37.9	381	32.6
A little	369	50.2	152	35.1	521	44.6
Not at all	12	1.6	7	1.6	19	1.6
Total*	709	96.4	421	97.2	1130	96.7

*Discrepancies between total responses and 100% represent the percentage that did not respond to the question.

TABLE 4

DISTRIBUTION OF AGES

Class Interval			Frequency
(Ages in yrs. and mos.)			
17-8	—	17-11	2
17-4	—	17-7	11
17-0	—	17-3	23
16-8	—	16-11	30
16-4	—	16-7	46
16-0	—	16-3	90
15-8	—	15-11	238
15-4	—	15-7	291
15-0	—	15-3	271
14-8	—	14-11	100
14-4	—	14-7	36
14-0	—	14-3	13
13-8	—	13-11	6
13-4	—	13-7	1

N = 1,158
Mean = 15 yrs., 6.7 mos.
Median = 15 yrs., 5.1 mos.
Mode = 15 yrs., 6.0 mos.

TABLE 5

SECTIONS OF DAILY NEWSPAPERS READ MOST FREQUENTLY BY HIGH SCHOOL STUDENTS

	Comics %	Sports %	Gen'l. News %	Local News %	Ads. %	Crime %	Eds. %
Boys	56.5	62.0	47.8	36.1	32.9	35.0	15.5
Girls	54.0	15.9	35.3	33.5	41.3	29.6	13.9
Both	55.6	44.9	43.2	35.1	36.0	33.0	14.9

TABLE 6

DISTRIBUTION OF IQ SCORES OF SECOND YEAR HIGH SCHOOL STUDENTS

IQ Scores	Boys (N=686) Freq.	Girls (N=404) Freq.	Both (N=1090) Freq.
160-169	1	0	1
150-159	3	1	4
140-149	12	6	18
130-139	29	8	37
120-129	52	25	77
110-119	125	60	185
100-109	171	75	246
90-99	161	89	250
80-89	62	78	140
70-79	50	54	104
60-69	17	8	25
50-59	3	0	3
Mean	103.1	98.2	101.2
Median	102.9	97.0	100.9
Mode	105.0	95.0	95.0

GRAPHS

Graphs are actually a kind of illustration and would be included in the list of illustrations. They may be placed on separate sheets of paper or be part of the page of text. In either case, the pages are numbered consecutively. The graphs are numbered consecutively with Arabic numerals. The rules for numbering and captions are the same as for tables. Graphs are generally line, bar, or picture graphs.

Graphs, as well as tables, serve a useful function when they are used as an aid to the text. They are incorporated for the convenience of the reader and should be clear, concise, and easy to comprehend. In the case of picture graphs, the writer must supply a legend.

ILLUSTRATIONS

In addition to the graphs mentioned, illustrations may consist of blueprints, pictures, diagrams, original drawings, maps, photographs, and generally anything that illustrates the text. The rules governing the use of illustrations are the same as those for tables. They should serve a definite purpose and should be placed as close to the text they illustrate as possible. The placement, numbering, writing of captions, and pagination are the same as for tables. All graphs and illustrations are included in the list of illustrations. If a paper contains a large number of graphs, you may then make a separate list.

Not all papers require the inclusion of tables, graphs, and/or illustrations. You should exercise the utmost discretion when incorporating these aids, for the overuse or improper use of them will weaken rather than strengthen the overall effect of the paper. You must remember at all times that your primary purpose is to present a scholarly discussion of your research, using pictorial aids only when necessary to aid the reader's comprehension of the text.

Chapter Eleven

The Final Manuscript

Before you are ready to type your final manuscript, you will have written your first draft of the complete paper including footnotes, table of contents, list of tables, bibliography, and appendices. Furthermore, you will have edited these drafts (the plural is used because it is assumed that there were several revisions—especially for style— which necessitated the rewriting of the first or "rough" draft either in part or completely) for any structural, mechanical, or content errors. In addition, you will have supplied a title that is concise and descriptive of the contents; and you will have checked your footnotes, bibliography, illustrations, and all other reference notes for accuracy. Once all this has been done, you are ready to prepare the final manuscript.

GENERAL DIRECTIONS

All dissertations and theses, and most research papers, must be typed, either on a word processor or a typewriter. Regardless of whether you prepare your own paper or pay a service to do it for you, you will be held responsible for any and all errors in the final manuscript.

Computer

A word processor and good-quality printer will give you a professional-looking manuscript. It will also simplify many tasks, such as footnotes and pagination. However, you should not engage in the creative use of different fonts or character sizes.

Typewriter

If you don't have access to a computer, then you will have to type your paper. The typewriter should be in good working order. The ribbon should retain a sufficient amount of ink for a uniformly clear imprint. When the subject matter requires the use of special characters, such as mathematical symbols, you must either use a typewriter containing these characters or have the paper typed professionally. These characters should not be inked in. You should use a good grade of bond paper. Erasable bond is highly recommended, for it will permit use of a pencil eraser without leaving smudges. Only white paper must be used.

Margins

Margins on all four sides of the paper should be equal. Since the paper will be stapled or bound on the left, the space taken up by the binding must be added to that margin. The top and bottom margins must be constant.

Alignment

Although word processors enable the writer to justify the right margin, it is not recommended for research papers. Use left alignment.

Spacing

The body of the manuscript—with the exception of footnotes, bibliographical entries, and quotations set off from the text—is double spaced. Other rules to be followed are:

1. All chapters and other divisions begin on a new page regardless of how much space is left on the preceding page.

2. On title pages of chapters and other divisions, the chapter number (e.g., CHAPTER III) is centered, eight lines from the top edge of the paper.

3. On all other pages, the page number is centered at the top edge of the paper and enclosed in dashes.

4. Following the chapter number, the title of the chapter is centered two lines below the chapter designation.

5. Three lines below the chapter title, the text begins.

6. All paragraphs should be indented one tab space from the margin.

7. All footnote entries are to be single-spaced with double spaces between the entries.

8. All quotations set off from the text and indented left and right are single-spaced.

9. All bibliographical entries are single-spaced with double spaces between the entries.

Footnotes

All footnotes should appear at the bottom of the page that they refer to. When a footnote entry is so long that it must be continued on the following page, the entry should be begun immediately following the place where it is referred to in the text and continued until the bottom margin. The remainder of the note is then continued on the next page in the footnote area (below the horizontal line) preceding any footnotes for that page. The continuation should not be indicated by any such statements as "continued on next page," or "continued." Only one footnote entry should appear on any one line.

Half-title page

Major divisions (e.g., parts, sections, appendices) are generally introduced by a half-title page—a sheet that contains the part number and title centered on the page and typed in uppercase letters throughout. Half-title pages are numbered with the rest of the paper but the page number is not placed on the page.

Proofreading

The final manuscript must be proofread very carefully. This means you will read the manuscript and the draft simultaneously, making sure there are no differences between the two. It is important to proofread your manuscript yourself, and do not just rely on the spell checker. A computer is no substitute for the human eye. For instance, the spell checker would not detect any errors in the sentence, "Due ewe sea any miss steaks hear?"

COLLATING

Once the paper has been carefully proofread, it is ready to be collated. Be sure to place a blank sheet following the title page and another blank sheet after the last page of the paper. The paper should then be fastened along the left-hand margin with two or three staples. If you so desire, you may enclose the manuscript in a plain manila or thesis folder. When a folder is used, the title of the paper and the writer's name should appear on the cover.

The research project is now complete, the paper is written, and, hopefully, you have found that it was a truly rewarding experience that not only made you keenly aware of a new aspect in the field but also whetted your appetite for further research.

Chapter Twelve

The Shorter Theme

It is generally assumed that before one undertakes to write a researched thesis paper, they have mastered the art of writing the shorter theme or the essay. Here again it must be stressed that, theoretically at least, you are not writing solely to fulfill a course requirement; such themes often tend to be rather sterile. It is hoped that you are writing because you have something to say; something you need to communicate. And communication is the only valid reason for writing. In this sense, you are an artist who chooses pen and paper rather than canvas and paint with which to express your thoughts and ideas. Although you may choose various modes of written expression—poem, short story, play, mood piece—this chapter will focus on the expository essay, that form of written expression that you will probably use most often.

TOPIC LIMITATION

Topic selection should not present a major problem. At best, the topic has been in your mind for a long time, and you are most anxious to get your ideas and thoughts on paper so that others can share your thinking; or at worst, your instructor has assigned the topic to you. The main problem, however, that you will confront is how to limit the topic, but before you can do that, there are several factors you must consider.

Purpose or objective

Before you begin to write—or outline your paper, for that matter—you must be certain of your purpose or objective. Do you simply want to inform your readers, or do you want to persuade or convince them to think along certain lines? Perhaps your objective is to move-to-action, to get your readers to follow a course, or perhaps your aim is simply to entertain? Certainly, these aims are not mutually exclusive, and it is conceivable that an effective theme may incorporate all of these objectives. However, one of these objectives should be dominant because it will determine the overall organization, diction, and tone of the theme. For example, the move-to-action theme must be much more forceful and dynamic than the persuasive theme, becuase although both will attempt to convince the reader, the former must get her to act whereas the latter is content with the reader's passive acceptance of an idea.

Audience

To be certain, the audience—the readers for whom you are writing—may help to determine your objective. But the audience serves a much more important function: it will determine your level of language, your diction, the degree of difficulty of the subject matter, and the intensity and extensity of the theme. You must ascertain the age of your audience, its educational and/or intellectual level, its knowledge of the subject matter, its interests, and its prejudices. Each of these will affect not only your topic limitation but also your overall approach.

Time limitation

The amount of time you are given to write your paper is also extremely important. A paper that must be produced within the confines of a 50-minute class period cannot be as extensive—or intensive—as a paper that can be worked on for several days. The same applies to word limitation, for these both are restrictive measures that demand topic limitation more so than any other factors.

Once you are aware of all the aforementioned factors, you are ready to limit your topic, keeping uppermost in your mind that you are obligated to say something useful and not just fill up space with words. Therefore, if you want to write about women's rights, you cannot deal with the subject in its entirety within the limitation of a 1,000-word paper. Therefore, you must limit your topic. Depending on your audience and your own knowledge of the subject, you might limit the topic to "the equality of women in the professions," or limit it further to "the equality of women in law." The important factor is that the limitation permits you to say something in depth, something that will not be a waste of the reader's time.

OUTLINING

Once you have decided on your topic limitation, your objective, and collected all of your information, you are ready to begin your outline. The outline is perhaps the most essential step in the writing process, for it permits you to see at a glance whether the paper will be unified.

The thesis statement, or the statement of purpose, is the focal point of the outline. It states concisely your objective. It is important, therefore, that you give careful thought to writing this statement, revising it as often as necessary until you are certain that it encompasses your aim for the paper. Under no circumstance are you to begin outlining before you have set down your thesis statement and are certain that it is an accurate statement of your aim.

The thesis statement should be phrased as a statement and not as a question. If the topic is "the equality of women in law," you might formulate your statement as follows:

Thesis statement: In law, more so than in any other profession, women have equal opportunities with men.

This statement will now set the tone for your paper. You must now proceed to prove this thesis. However, before you can begin to outline, you must know what basic method of development you will use.

As in paragraph development, which is discussed later in this chapter, themes should be developed either by instances and examples, comparison and/or contrast, cause and effect, definition, anecdote, or steps in a process. Although these methods of development are not mutually exclusive, one of them should dominate. It is that dominant method that will affect the outline. For example, if the basic method is instances and examples, then the outline must contain instances and/or examples that will effectively substantiate the thesis. If, on the other hand, the method is anecdote, then the outline must contain a detailed occurrence that will, through the telling of the anecdote, substantiate the thesis.

In outlining, you have two forms from which to choose: the Harvard (formal) outline and the informal outline. The former is an extremely flexible format that can be employed as readily for a short theme or for a book whereas the latter can be employed only for the short theme.

The Harvard outline follows a rigid format: Roman numerals indicate major divisions (in the longer paper, they can indicate parts of the paper; in the shorter paper, paragraphs); uppercase letters indicate subdivisions; Arabic numerals further subdivisions. For example:

I.
II.
III.
    A.
    B.
    C.
        1.
        2.
            a.
            b.
            c.
            d.
                (1)
                (2)
                    (a)
                    (b)
IV.

The indentation must be exactly as above. Furthermore, items should be expressed in parallel form. For example, if item I. is a prepositional phrase, then all Roman numeral items must be prepositional phrases; if A. is an infinitive, then all uppercase items under the same Roman numeral must be infinitives. Also, there must be at least two subtopics (or none), for subtopics are subdivisions, and no item can be divided into fewer than two parts.

Although the formal outline may, at first glance, seem too formal and stiff, it is a form that you would do well to master. It will allow you to see at a glance whether you are developing your thesis or not. The informal outline is just that—extremely informal. Here you just jot down in phrase form all those items that you think will help you prove your thesis. After you have completed the listing, you determine whether each item will help prove the thesis. If not, the item is eliminated. The remaining items are then arranged in logical order.

Regardless of which type of outline you use, you must recognize that once the outline has been completed, you must follow it without any deviation. Should you feel compelled to deviate in the middle, do so only if you revise the outline entirely. An outline that is not scrupulously followed serves no useful purpose.

PARAGRAPHING

Before dealing with the actual writing of the theme, it might be well to digress at this point to discuss paragraph development and organization, for the paragraph is a multi-paragraphed theme in miniature where each paragraph is comparable to each sentence in the paragraph.

The expository paragraph consists of the development of a single idea through a series of related sentences. The idea is introduced by a topic sentence that sets forth the main idea of the paragraph. It is developed through a series of related sentences that prove the topic statement; and it is ended with a concluding sentence. The effective paragraph must be unified and coherent. Let us look at each of these characteristics individually.

Topic sentence

The topic sentence encompasses the gist of the paragraph and sets its tone. As such, it usually comes at the beginning of the paragraph, although it could come in the middle or at the end. There are two types of topic sentences that you can employ: the direct statement and the indirect statement. For example:

Direct: Student action has contributed substantially to the elimination of formal undergraduate requirements. In developing this paragraph, you must show specifically how student activism has contributed to the elimination of formal undergraduate requirements.

Indirect: Recently I had an interesting chat with an educator friend of mine concerning the future of television. This paragraph will focus on the future of educational television. The reference to "educator friend of mine" implied the limitation.

Regardless of which type of topic sentence you use, it must be vivid, stimulating, and exciting, for it will determine whether or not the reader reads the rest of the paragraph. You must always remember that you are striving to retain the reader's attention and interest. The reader, unlike the listener who remains throughout the speech because common courtesy demands it, is free to stop reading at any time, and once she stops reading the selection, there is nothing you can do to regain her attention.

Methods of paragraph development

It is in the body of the paragraph where you prove your topic sentence. If the development is weak or incomplete, then you have failed to make your point. Therefore, it is essential that the paragraph be adequately developed. A two- or three-sentence paragraph is comparable to a very skimpy sandwich—very unsatisfying. Although the bottom slice of bread, like the topic sentence, supports the sandwich meats, it is the sandwich meats that make the sandwich worthwhile. So it is with the paragraph. The tastiness of the paragraph is, in part, determined by the method of development you use.

Instances and/or examples

In the paragraph of instances and examples (instances are actual occurrences; examples are fictitious events) you will select those instances or examples that will substantiate your topic sentence. You must be careful not to use too few instances—leaving the reader unconvinced—nor use too many—leaving the reader bored.

Sample paragraph—instances and/or examples

Live television has many hazards. During a recent news broadcast, for instance, the audience was shown film clips of a beauty pageant as the newscaster introduced scenes from a political convention. In another broadcast, the announcer had a coughing fit just as she was lighting the cigarette that she was advertising. And perhaps most noteworthy of all was the case of the famed chanteuse whose strap broke just as she was reaching for that high note. Yes, live television certainly has its hazards.

Comparison and/or contrast

Most significant here is that the topic sentence must state or imply that a comparison (similarities of two or more items) or contrast (differences) will be made. At no time can you begin discussing *Macbeth* and then later in the paragraph discuss *Hamlet*, unless you have so stated in the topic sentence. Such a paragraph will lack unity.

There are two ways to develop a paragraph of comparison and/or contrast. In the first instance, you will state all you have to say about *Macbeth* and then state all the comparable items about *Hamlet*. In the second instance, you will follow each statement about *Macbeth* with a comparable statement about *Hamlet*. This could be illustrated as follows:

Topic sentence —	Macbeth and Hamlet
Development —	Macbeth; Macbeth; Macbeth Hamlet; Hamlet; Hamlet
Concluding sentence —	Macbeth and Hamlet

or:

Topic sentence —	Macbeth and Hamlet
Development —	Macbeth; Hamlet Macbeth; Hamlet Macbeth; Hamlet
Concluding sentence —	Macbeth and Hamlet

Sample paragraph—comparison and/or contrast

Writing is very similar to painting. Both the artist and the writer have something they feel an unrelenting urge to express; something they must communicate. The artist makes use of her canvas, her paints, and her brushes. The writer employs her paper, her words, and her pen. Whereas the artist makes effective use of colors and brush strokes, so does the writer through her careful use of words and syntax. Although the finished product is different, both artist and writer have expressed their feelings and, hopefully, communicated them to others.

Cause and effect

Depending on the content, the paragraph of cause and effect can consist of a topic sentence that is a statement of cause followed by a series of sentences that indicate the effects of said cause, or a topic sentence that is a statement of the effect (the end result) of several causes. In a sense, this method of paragraph development is nothing more than a paragraph of instances and examples where the instances are either causes or effects.

Definition

Occasionally, you may need to define a term or concept within a longer paper. As a rule, such a term would be an abstract rather than a concrete term, for if the definition can readily be found in the dictionary, there is little need to devote a paragraph defining it. Hence, the paragraph of definition should never begin with "According to the dictionary. . . ."

The term can be defined in several different ways. One way is to compare or contrast it to another item or concept. Another way is to define it through instances or examples. A third way is by an anecdote that illustrates the concept. It is even conceivable to use a combination of these methods.

Anecdote

An anecdote is little more than a sustained instance or example. The paragraph of anecdote basically employs the narrative technique wherein you recall an occurrence (or fabricates one) that will substantiate your topic statement. It is, incidentally, this method of development that lends itself most readily to having the topic sentence appear at the end of the paragraph.

Sample paragraph—anecdote

> Contrary to popular belief, not all teachers are insensitive to their students' needs. I well remember an incident that happened many years ago in an old dilapidated elementary school in Brooklyn. Having arrived from Europe only days before and being unable to speak any English, I was enrolled in school, but in first grade rather than in the fourth where I belonged. I felt completely ill at ease: the kids stared at me, this gangling kid who was too big for the seat and who could speak only German. However, the teacher's warm smile, her attempts to communicate with me in her high school German, her spending her lunch hour and the recess period with me soon made me feel

comfortable in these new surroundings. It was her warmth and sensitivity that made me want to keep going to school and learn the language and the customs of this new country.

Steps-in-a-process

Whereas the preceding paragraphs are generally developed logically, either in ascending or descending order of importance, the paragraph of steps-in-a-process is developed chronologically. This paragraph is geared primarily to explaining the step-by-step procedure to be followed in fulfilling any given task. Your main objective is to be sure that anyone reading the paragraph will be able to accomplish the task described without any difficulty.

Sample paragraph—steps-in-a-process

Almost anyone can learn how to boil water. First of all, supply yourself with the following materials: a metal container approximately six inches deep and five inches in diameter, preferably with a handle; water; a stove or hot plate; and matches or an electric outlet. Once you have assembled all these materials, you are ready for step two. Take the metal container in hand and proceed to the water supply, filling the pot within one inch of the rim. After turning off the water supply, proceed to the stove and place the container on the burner, being careful not to spill the water. Now light the burner so that the temperature will reach 450 degrees, watch the water carefully and note when it begins to bubble. As soon as the water bubbles furiously, the water is boiled. At this time, turn off the supply of heat; you have just boiled water.

Combination

None of these methods are mutually exclusive and, hence, can be used in combination. For example, the paragraph of comparison could employ instances; the paragraph of definition could employ contrasts and instances. It is possible, although not probable, that a paragraph could combine all methods here discussed.

Concluding sentence

Each paragraph must have a concluding sentence, a sentence that lets the reader know you have finished. At no time, however, should that sentence begin with "In conclusion," for that would be an admission of ineffectiveness of the ending. The ending should be a logical conclusion that says, in essence, to the reader: "Look, I have just proven my topic statement."

Unity and coherence

Unity and coherence are essential in paragraph development. Unity is achieved by determining that each sentence within the paragraph is relevant to the topic sentence. That is, each sentence is a *further* development and substantiation of the topic sentence. Coherence is the logical connection of the sentences to each other. Coherence can be achieved through a variety of techniques (*see page 41*).

To assure unity and coherence in the paragraph, you should ask yourself whether each sentence is relevant to the topic statement and whether it adds something to that which has already been said. If the answer is yes for each sentence in the paragraph, then the paragraph is unified. In addition, you should also ask yourself if each sentence logically follows that which precedes it and if it is properly joined to the thought that follows. If the answer is yes, then the paragraph is coherent.

You might want to compare your paragraph to a train. The locomotive is the topic sentence that gives the train (paragraph) its direction. Each car is a sentence that must belong with the rest of the train, for it must go where the locomotive goes, and each car must be properly coupled to the car before and after it. And, finally, the caboose is the concluding sentence that indicates that it is the last car in the train.

INTRODUCTORY PARAGRAPH

The introductory paragraph is, perhaps, the most important part of the entire theme and deserving of the greatest effort. It is this paragraph that will determine whether the reader will read the essay. A dull, boring opening, such as, "In this paper I will discuss. . .," will prompt the reader to turn to another selection immediately. The introduction must be stimulating, vivid, alive, causing the reader to be anxious to read on. In addition, of course, this paragraph should contain the essence of the thesis, an implication of the method of development, and set the tone of the paper. On a purely mechanical level, each developmental sentence in the introductory paragraph could serve as a topic sentence for each paragraph within the theme.

DEVELOPMENT

Once the reader's appetite has been whetted by the introductory paragraph, you must now strive to retain the reader's interest with every single paragraph. You must always keep uppermost in your mind that the reader is fickle, that she can stop reading at anytime she becomes bored, and there is absolutely no way you can bring her back to the paper. Keep asking yourself: "What is so good about my paper that the reader will prefer reading it to all the others available to her?"

The outline and the method of development will determine the body of the paper. The paper of comparison and/or contrast will develop its thesis by comparing and/or contrasting two characters, ideas, or events. To be certain, such a method of development does not imply that every paragraph within the paper will be one of comparison and/or contrast. It is very likely that some paragraphs could be developed by instances and examples, some by cause and effect, some by anecdote, and some by comparison.

Again, on a purely mechanical level, each paragraph in the theme could be the development of a sentence in the introductory paragraph:

Introductory paragraph:

> Topic sentence
> Sentence 1
> Sentence 2
> Sentence 3
> Sentence 4
> Concluding sentence

Development:

> Paragraph 1: Topic sentence = sentence 1
>
>> Sentence A
>> Sentence B
>> Sentence C
>> Concluding sentence
>
> Paragraph 2: Topic sentence = sentence 2
>
>> Sentence D
>> Sentence E
>> Sentence F
>> Sentence G
>> Concluding sentence
>
> Paragraph 3: Topic sentence = sentence 3
> Paragraph 4: Topic sentence = sentence 4

However, it should be remembered that such a purely mechanical method of development could create a very dull and stilted paper.

CONCLUDING PARAGRAPH

The concluding paragraph lets the reader know in no uncertain terms that the argument has been presented in its entirety and that you are finished. The well-organized argument comes to its conclusion logically and naturally. If you find yourself having to say "in conclusion" or "to sum up," or any other comparable phrase, then you are, in fact, suggesting that your ending is weak. Although a rephrasing of the introductory paragraph is better than no ending at all, the test of the good ending is simple: If it were at the bottom of the page, would the reader be tempted to turn to the next page for the continuation? If no, then the ending was strong, forceful, and final. You must remember that the ending is the last thought that you leave with your reader.

UNITY AND COHERENCE

The concepts of unity and coherence discussed for the paragraph apply here as well. Just as each paragraph must have unity, so must the theme as a whole. You must be positive that each paragraph is a further development of the thesis stated in the introduction. You must also be certain that there is proper transition from one paragraph to the next, that paragraphs follow each other in logical sequence, that the point of view has been maintained, and that tangential and irrelevant ideas have not been introduced.[1] To achieve all this may require several drafts before you are ready to write your final paper. Good writing is not accidental nor is it easy; it is a time-consuming, difficult undertaking, but one that, when well done, can be highly rewarding. What greater thrill can there be than to communicate one's ideas, thoughts, or feelings to others?

TITLE

Although the title of the paper may be supplied last, it is an integral and important part of the paper. It entices the reader to choose to read the paper. It either states or implies the content, and it sets the tone. Without the title, the paper is incomplete. Therefore, it becomes imperative that you give careful consideration to the selection of an appropriate title, one that is concise, interesting, and holds the promise of great things to come.

Writing only to fulfill course requirements will not offer you much pleasure or satisfaction. The well-written theme is one that you are proud of. It is a theme that you will not be ashamed to have read by your peers or have published under your name.

---

[1]For a detailed discussion on coherence and unity, point of view, and some aspects of style, see Chapter Six, pp. 35-40.

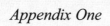

Appendix One

Sample Research Paper University of Chicago Style

LITERATURE AND BIOGRAPHY
By Harry Teitelbaum

English-education 311.13

Hofstra University
January 15, 2003

PREFACE

I have been troubled for years with the very common practice in English literature texts, especially anthologies used in the secondary schools, of giving detailed biographical and social background of the writer and the work before the student has even had the opportunity of reading the selection. Some of these texts, particularly in the realm of poetry, will go as far as to "suggest" the "true" interpretation of the poem. What happens so often, of course, is that the student will simply re-state the editor's point of view rather than attempt to formulate one of his own. Hence, both the teacher and the student are never quite certain whether the student has obtained anything from the work itself.

To an extent this also holds true for the biographical information supplied. If the student is told before reading that the author tends to write about certain subjects or tends to take a certain point of view, the reader's own interpretation will, no doubt, be strongly influenced, either consciously or subconsciously. His interpretation will become prejudiced in favor of the one he has read, especially since the average high school student lacks confidence in his interpretive ability to begin with.

The problem, then, is what to do about it. First, it is extremely difficult to ask the student to ignore what precedes the selection, for even when the biographical information appears at the end of the text, the student is quick to realize that this presents a "clue" to him that will take the burden of interpretation off his shoulders. Second, trained as so many of us have been in the biographical-critical and historical-critical approach, we will tend to supply the student with this background as motivation for reading the literary work. In order to see what can be done about this, I am interested in determining the thinking of the critics on this subject.

-ii-

Aside from studying the biography of an author as an entity in itself without relating the biographical aspects to his writing, there seem to be two approaches to literature and biography. One is the use of the poem[1] as a clue to the author's life, and the second is the use of the known facts of the author's life as an aid in the interpretation of the poem.

Insofar as I am concerned, the discussion of the first approach, i.e., that the poem is a source of the author's biography, is purely academic, especially in those instances where no biographical proof exists outside of the poem. The analysis, for example, of Shakespeare's works by critics who have argued that, based on his works, Shakespeare must have been a lawyer, a soldier, a teacher, a farmer, etc., is pure academic guesswork. The critic who feels that the author must have based everything on personal experience strikes me as being somewhat naive. Ellen Terry, according to Wellek and Warren, gave the crushing reply to all this literary detective work when she argued that, by the same criteria, Shakespeare must have been a woman.[2]

Yet this approach was and is being used. Robert Gittlings, in *John Keats: The Living Year* (1954), presents some new information about the circumstances in which Keats produced the poems he wrote between September 1818 and September 1819. He suggests that the "Bright Star" sonnet was originally written not to Fanny but to Mrs. Isabella Jones.[3] Although this may alter our view of Keats' life and his mind, it will not alter our view of his poetry. Similar kinds of literary-biographical detective work was carried out by others as well, among them Miss Wade, in her *Life of Traherne*, Virginia Moore in *Eager Death of Emily Bronte*, and numerous others in the many works about the lives of the Brontes, Shakespeare, Gray, Donne, Burns, and others. Perhaps the most fascinating of all these works is Frank Harris' *The Man*

---

[1]The term *poem* in this paper refers to all literary works.

[2]Rene Wellek and Austin Warren, *Theory of Literature,* rev. ed. (New York, 1956), p. 67, citing Ellen Terry.

[3]David Daiches, *Critical Approaches to Literature,* 2nd ed. (Essex, England, 1981), p. 338.

-1-

-2-

Shakespeare and His Tragic Life-Story. Here Harris "proves" that Shakespeare ". . .painted himself at full-length, not once, but twenty times, at as many different periods of his life."[4] And an interesting account of Shakespeare's life it is, but how much truth there is in this biographical account is highly doubtful. Harris seems to work under the complete assumption, which to me is unacceptable, that the author bases everything on personal experience.

In answer to E.M.W. Tillyard's *Milton* (1930), where he treats *Paradise Lost* as the record of the poet's state of mind during the period when he wrote it, C.S. Lewis counters that *Paradise Lost* was not about Milton's state of mind, but about Satan, Adam and Eve, the fall of Man, and similar subjects. Lewis cannot accept the concept that to read poetry well is to have a true idea of the poet, while to read poetry poorly is to have a false idea of him. He feels that when we read poetry as "poetry should be read," we have before us no representation which claims to be the poet, and frequently no representation of ". . .a *man*, a *character*, or a *personality* at all."[5]

Using the *Prelude* as an example, Lewis argues that if we take Wordsworth's poem as a whole, the appreciation of it as poetry does not include the knowledge that it is autobiographical. "A process of human development, that is, a particular man growing up, is presented to us; that this man is, or is intended to be, Wordsworth himself, we learn from literary history — unless we are so simple as to suppose that the use of the first person settles the question."[6] We do not know whether the story of the sonnets was Shakespeare's own story (Mr. Harris to the contrary); we do not know whether Milton really grieved for the death of Mr. King; and if we know that Shelley really met Keats, we do not know it". . . in and by appreciating *Adonais*."[7]

---

[4]Frank Harris, The Man Shakespeare and His Tragic Life-Story (New York, 1909), p. x.

[5]C.S. Lewis, "The Personal Heresy in Criticism," *Essays and Studies by Members of the English Association,* Collected by D. Nichol Smith (Oxford, 1934), XIX, 9.

[6]*Ibid.,* p. 13.

-3-

Wellek and Warren too are in agreement with this point of view when they state that it is not self-evident that a writer needs to be in a tragic mood to write tragedies or that he writes comedies when he feels pleased with life. There is simply no proof for the sorrows of Shakespeare. He cannot be made responsible for the views of Timon or Macbeth on life. "The relationship between the private life and the work is not a simple relationship of cause and effect."[8]

Lewis tends to explain away, in part, the personal dogma by recognizing that this personal view offers obvious advantages. Very few care for beauty; but anyone can be interested in gossip. "To such people any excuse for shutting up the terrible books with all the lines and lines of verse in them and getting down to the snug or piquant details of human life, will always be welcome."[9] But, yet, he feels that there is a deeper reason than this:

> The personal dogma springs from an inability that most moderns feel to make up their minds between two alternatives. A materialist, and a spiritual, theory of the universe are both equally fatal to it; but in the coming and going of the mind between the two it finds its opportunity. For the typical modem critic is usually a halfhearted materialist. He accepts, or thinks he accepts, that picture of the world that popularized science gives him. He thinks that everything except the buzzing electrons is subjective fancy; and he therefore believes that all poetry must come out of the poet's head and express (of course) his pure, uncontaminated, undivided "personality," because outside of the poet's head there is nothing but the interplay of blind forces. But he forgets that if materialism is true, there is nothing else inside the poet's head either. For a consistent materialism, the poetless poetry. . . and the most seemingly self-expressive "human document," are equally accidental results of the impersonal and irrational causes. And if this is so, if the sensation. . .which we call "enjoying poetry" in no case betokens that we are really in the presence of purpose and spirituality, then there is no foothold left for the personal heresy.[10]

---

[7]Loc. cit.

[8]Wellek, *op. cit.,* p. 65.

[9]Lewis, *op. cit.,* p. 27.

[10]*Ibid.,* pp. 27-28.

-4-

Although I am more inclined to agree with this point of view, there is something to be said for Tillyard's rebuttal to Lewis wherein he contends that although the poet may, as T.S. Eliot claims, surrender himself wholly to the work to be done, the paradox consists that the poet, as a result of self-surrender, often produces the most personal and characteristic work. "The more the poet experiences this abandonment of personality," Tillyard states, "the more likely is the reader to hail the poet's characteristic, unmistakable self . . . Nor will it make the poet any less personal, if he carefully avoids every vestige of private emotion, if he seeks the utmost justification. On the contrary,. . .[this] will express all the more clearly. . .the characteristic lines of the poet's mental pattern."[11]

Of course, insofar as I can see, this does not negate the basic problem of the critic "reading into" the poem. For an attempt to determine the mental processes and personal experiences of the poet based solely on the poem is still a dangerous and highly questionable, albeit interesting, undertaking.

The strongest argument I have come across favoring the use of poems as materials for biography is that of Leslie A. Fiedler who feels that the antibiographical arguments were in reaction to Romantic subjectivity. In his article, "Archetype and Signature: A Study of the Relationship between Biography and Poetry," Fiedler presents the argument that antibiographists felt that the Romantic approach attempted to prove that the work of art was

> . . .*nothing* but the personality of the Genius behind it or the sum total of its genetic factors. . .The antibiographists offered. . .the "intrinsic" approach, which turned out. . .to be another *nothing but* under its show of righteous indignation, namely, the contention that a poem was *nothing but* "words," and its analysis therefore properly *nothing but* a study of syntax and semantics. Any attempt to illuminate a poem by reference to its author's life came, therefore, to be regarded with horror.[12]

---

[11]E.M.W. Tillyard, "The Personal Heresy in Criticism: A Rejoinder," *Essays and Studies by Members of the English Association,* collected by George Cookson (Oxford, 1935), XX, 13-14.

[12]Leslie A. Fiedler, "Archetype and Signature: A Study of the Relationship between Biography and Poetry." *Sewanee Review,* 60:254, 1952.

-5-

He is further opposed to the concept of "A poem should not mean but be." Also he objects to the argument that the poem is self-contained and nothing exists outside of it (e.g., How long was Hamlet in Wittenberg?).

These, then, are the major arguments presented for and against the use of the poem as a biographical source. Interesting though this literary detective work may be, it still is nothing more than an academic exercise which will never offer any conclusive proof. For I am in complete agreement with Wellek and Warren when they point out that "the work of art is not a document for biography."[13]

The second approach to literature — the use of the *known* facts of the author's life as an aid in the interpretation of the poem — perhaps has greater validity, for here one may find information that *may* prove to be useful for a better understanding of the literary work. How valid, though, this approach is remains to be seen, for here, too, critics seem to stand divided.

Fiedler again strongly disagrees with the concept that biographical information is irrelevant to the understanding and evaluation of the poem. He is opposed to the point of view that deprives the poet of his right to explain his own poem or that challenges his claim to speak with final authority about his own work. He objects to the approach of the new critics that once the poem has been written, the author becomes just another reader. The concept that the author cannot protest against any interpretation if the poem is to be judged "successful" is, to Fiedler, absurd. Fiedler definitely does not object to the author discussing his "intentions" since, he feels, we can then judge the poem better. It is the bringing in from outside ". . .all kinds of rich relevancies and connecting them with the poem. . ." that makes it rich. Staying "inside the poem" will not permit this richness.[14]

According to Fiedler, the old biographists were unsuccessful because they failed to connect the facts with the work they presumed to illuminate. The proper use of biography, however, in conjunction with the work makes up the total meaning. It is this which will raise the meaning to a higher power.

---

[13]Welleck, *op. cit.,* p. 67.

[14]Fiedler, *op. cit.,* pp. 257-259.

-6-

Perhaps Fiedler's argument can be seen more clearly through an understanding of his definition of the poem, which he speaks of as *Archetype* and *Signature*. He defines *Archetype* as "any of the immemorial patterns of response to the human situation in its most permanent aspects: death, love, biological family, relation with Unknown. . .,".[15] *Signature* he defines as the ". . .sum total of individuating factors in a work, the Persona or Personality, through which the Archetype is rendered and which itself tends to become a subject as well as the means of the poem."[16] Literature, he feels, comes into existence at the moment a Signature is imposed upon the Archetype. Without the Signature, there is only a myth.

Fiedler admonishes his reader to connect the "poet and the poem, the lived and the made, the Signature and the Archetype. It is on the focus of the poetic personality," he states, "that *Dichtung* [poetry] and *Wahreit* [*sic*; truth] become one; and it is incumbent upon us, without surrendering our right to make useful distinctions, to seize the principle of that unity. 'Only connect!'"[17]

Most critics today shy away from taking either extreme position; that is, that biographical information is entirely extrinsic and hence has little, if any, value in the understanding and/or evaluation of a poem; and that biographical information is necessary to the complete understanding of the literary work. Most of the critics that I have thus far read take more of a middle-of-the-road point of view; that is, they will admit that biographical information can have certain value. Perhaps this comes in reaction to the feelings, as expressed by W.M. Frohock in an essay in *Strangers to This Ground* and cited by Granville Hicks, that "textual criticism is now triumphant in most of the universities. Biography is irrelevant; social background is irrelevant; nothing matters but the work of literature, and this the student scrutinizes with the care and precision of a microbiologist examining a segment of tissue."[18]

---

[15]*Ibid.,* pp. 261-262.

[16]*Ibid.,* p. 262.

[17]*Ibid.,* p. 273.

[18]Granville Hicks, "*Literary Horizons:* Gestation of a Brain Child," *Saturday Review*, 45:62, January 6, 1962.

-7-

Wellek and Warren, even though Hicks feels that they practice textual criticism with austerity, believe that, if used with discrimination, there is use in biographical study for it may explain a great many allusions or even words in an author's work.[19] However, Wellek and Warren continue to state that whatever the importance of biography in these respects, "it seems dangerous to ascribe to it any specifically critical importance. No biographical evidence can change or influence critical evaluation."[20]

Wellek and Warren are not alone in their beliefs. David Daiches feels that it is often useful and sometimes valuable to use biography and the work as a help in interpreting each other. However, he, too, limits this usefulness to interpretation and not for assessment:

> One could take the biography of a writer, as illustrated by the external events of his life and such things as letters and other confessional documents, and construct out of these a theory of the writer's personality — his conflicts, frustrations, traumatic experiences, neuroses, or whatever they happened to be — and use this theory in order to illuminate each one of his works. Or one can work back and forth between the life and the work, illuminating each by the other, noting from the biography certain crises reflected in the works, and seeing from the way they are reflected in the works what their real biographical meaning was. This is often dangerous, if highly stimulating, theorizing, and its relation to critical evaluation is, at most, very tenuous.[21]

Elizabeth Nitchie in *The Criticism of Literature* also expresses similar feelings. Although she feels, on one hand, that it is well for the critic to know the biography of the author for it will aid him in better understanding the work, on the other hand, she feels that interesting though this type of study may be,

---

[19]Wellek, *op. cit.*, p. 68. Fiedler illustrates this by using Donne's line from "Love's Alchemie": "they are but Mummy possesst." He points out that knowing of Donne's intimate relationship with his mother gives the reader cause to interpret this line that "women once possessed, turn out to be substitutes for the Mother who is the real end of our desiring." Fiedler, *op. cit.*, pp. 265-266.

The question though, as I see it, still remains: Does knowing this make it a better poem?

[20]Loc. cit.

[21]Daiches, *op. cit.,* p. 345.

-8-

the biography may well color and affect our evaluation, for "no man's literary work should be judged by his life."[22]

Louise Rosenblatt in *Literature as Exploration* finds that it may at times be necessary to place the literary work in the context of the life of the personality of the author since this may ". . .confirm for us more definitely those things that we sense in his work."[23] Knowledge about the author's life, she feels, and the literary influences acting upon him ". . .will create the need for understanding the intellectual and philosophical, the social and economic, conditions surrounding them."[24]

Perhaps differentiating between appreciation and/or understanding and criticism can solve part of this problem. Knowledge of the author's life may well help us in understanding and appreciating a work since without this biographical knowledge, elements in the poem may well elude us. Yet this knowledge will rarely if ever help us in evaluative criticism, in better seeing the work as it objectively is.

Even Tillyard sees the inherent danger in the mixture of biography and criticism. Although Tillyard finds that the danger may be in the reader using biography as an ". . .illegitimate short cut into the poet's mental pattern as revealed by his poems,"[25] something akin to using "a crib when reading a foreign text,"[26] I am more concerned with the reader arriving at an evaluation of the work that is based on nothing more than the author's intent or some biographical data which may have no bearing whatsoever on the poem.

Thus far, I have yet to find a forceful and valid argument for the use of biography as an important factor in the evaluation of a poem. Nor have I found anything to convince me that biographical knowledge prior to the reading of a poem is useful. Insofar as I am concerned, I share Professor Tillyard's fears

---

[22]Elizabeth Nitchie, *The Criticism of Literature* (New York, 1929), pp. 13-14.

[23]Louise M. Rosenblatt, *Literature as Exploration*, 5th ed. (New York, 1996), p. 137.

[24]*Ibid.*, p. 138.

[25]Tillyard, *op. cit.*, p. 16.

[26]*Ibid.*, pp. 16-17.

-9-

that the student may use this as a short cut, but I fear it for different reasons. I
am afraid that the student will read into the work things that are not there,
things that he will not be able to substantiate from his reading of the poem.
Basic understanding and appreciation should be derived from the literary work
itself, without the reader's awareness of the author's intent, because first, the
work must exist on its merits. Afterwards, perhaps, knowledge of the author's
biography may prove useful in that it may shed further light on the reading and
aid in greater understanding and appreciation. To this extent I will agree with
Granville Hicks: "To isolate the literary object is a valid method of attack, but to
leave it in isolation is a mistake"; ". . .anything that increases awareness is
good."[27]

[27]Hicks, *loc. cit.*

BIBLIOGRAPHY

Daiches, David. *Critical Approaches to Literature*. 2nd ed. Essex, England: Longman Group Ltd., 1981.

Fiedler, Leslie A. "Archetype and Signature: A Study of the Relationship between Biography and Poetry," *Sewanee Review*, 60:253-273. 1952.

Fishman, Solomon. *The Disinherited of Art, Writer and Background*. Los Angeles: University of California Press, 1953.

Harris, Frank. *The Man Shakespeare and His Tragic Life-Story*. New York: Mitchell Kennerley, 1909.

Hicks, Granville. "*Literary Horizons:* Gestation of a Brain Child," *Saturday Review*, 45:62. January 6, 1962.

_____. "*Literary Horizons:* The Newest Pamphleteers," *Saturday Review*, 44:23. November 11, 1961.

Lewis, C.S. "The Personal Heresy in Criticism," *Essays and Studies by Members of the English Association*. Collected by D. Nichol Smith. Oxford: The Clarendon Press, 1934. Vol. XIX, pp. 7-28.

Nitchie, Elizabeth. *The Criticism of Literature*. New York: The Macmillan Company, 1929.

Rosenblatt, Louise M. *Literature as Exploration*. 5th ed. New York: Modern Language Association of America, 1996.

Tillyard, E.M.W. "The Personal Heresy in Criticism, A Rejoinder," *Essays and Studies by Members of the English Association*. Collected by George Cookson. Oxford: The Clarendon Press, 1935. Vol XX, pp. 7-20.

Wellek, Rene and Austin Warren. *Theory of Literature*. Rev. ed. New York: Harcourt Brace, 1956. Chap. 7.

MLA STYLE

Alicia Perkins
Ms. R.O. Cooper
Senior English
14 January 2003

When Alzheimers Hits Home

As a reflection of the human condition, early literature includes references to "old timer's" disease. Perhaps Shakespeare's *King Lear* best describes the malady when he says to his daughter Cordelia and her husband:

I fear I am not in my perfect mind.
Methinks I should know you, and know this man;
Yet I am doubtful; for I am mainly ignorant
What place this is; and all the skill I have
Remembers not these garments; nor I know not
Where I did lodge last night. Do not laugh at me.
(4.7. 63-68)

Lear no doubt suffers from the irreversible brain deterioration known today as Alzheimer's Disease, or AD. Unnamed until 1906 when Alois Alzheimer described the condition ("Chronology" 625), AD, an organic disease that destroys brain cells, now affects up to 4 million Americans (You Are Not Alone). Within 50 years, predictions say that 14 million sufferers will face the fourth leading cause of death in America (ADRDA, Statistics I).

When a relative has AD, however, statistics, frightening or not, take a back seat. The disease referred to as the "dementing thief of minds and destroyer of personalities" (Leroux 2) so dramatically changes a loved one that families struggle to cope; and among family members, young people face unique problems. In the midst of striving to understand their own changing adolescent roles, they may also find themselves striving to understand a changing grandparent. They face a tough challenge both to understand and to deal with the grandparent's cognitive deterioration, communication impairments, and behavior modifications.

Any form of dementia, AD being the worst, involves the "loss or impairment of mental powers" (Mace 5). The impairment begins slowly, almost imperceptibly: forgetting names, words, and later, meals; being unable to make change, balance a checkbook, or learn anything new; getting lost; or forgetting the day or month. As the disease progresses, victims lose the ability to track time, even confusing day and night. As a result, they may want to dress at odd hours, want to leave as soon as they arrive somewhere, think they have been left alone for days or weeks when it is only for a few minutes ("Stages of AD" 16-17). "For the person with a memory impairment, life may be like constantly coming into the middle of a movie—one has no idea what happened just before what is happening now" (Mace 24). Perhaps Mary's case helps explain the loss of cognitive powers:

> Mary gradually lost the ability to make sense out of what her eyes and ears told her. Noises and confusion made her feel panicky. She couldn't understand, they couldn't explain, and often panic overwhelmed her. She worried about her things: a chair, and the china that had belonged to her mother. They said they had told her over and over, but she could not remember where her things had gone. Perhaps someone had stolen them. She had lost so much. What things she did have, she hid, but then she forgot where she hid them (Mace 3).

When a grandparent or other relative shows cognitive deficits, families face the frustration that in spite of the fact that grandmother does not look sick, she is. She may lose the ability to dial the telephone, use a can opener, put on a sweater, tie her shoes, or distinguish between detergent and mouthwash. In this condition, "even the most minute change [in routine or environment] may lead to additional confusion and disorientation in the patient" (Powell 145), changes the patient" (Powell 145), changes like additional noise, additional people, or strangers. When grandmother suffers from cognitive deficits, young people generally encounter more frustration than do other family members, for teens often like loud music, boisterous groups of peers, and crowds of friends over for an evening or weekend. If grandmother lives with the family, her reaction may be rage, restlessness, confusion, or agitation. So, how does a teen cope with grandmother's condition?

Research suggests that many times young people "have clever ideas about how to solve problems that the rest of the family may not have thought of" (Mace 187). Because of their youth and resilience, once teens come to grips with the reality of grandmother's condition, they often know how to help. They seem to know intuitively, for instance, how to modify a task, to simplify rather than change it. The simplification lets grandmother continue a relatively normal life. At the same time, teens can laugh when they find the curtain rod in the freezer (Powell 135). Their youth often renders them more sympathetic than older members of the family, and they readily recognize that "the patient must be treated with kindness and dignity while at the same time being watched like a young child . . . [needing] overt signs of love and warmth" (Tanner and Shaw 97-98).

Teens can be supportive, too, by spending time with grandmother, taking her for a walk or for a visit with an old friend; helping her keep up social activities as much as possible; helping her feel needed; reading to her or getting talking books or records for her; taking her to the zoo, museum, park, or shopping center; and naming visitors and relatives to help her recognize and remember them (Cohen 148). Teens can compensate for grandmother's cognitive deficits by verbalizing their own sensory perceptions—pointing out the sunset, birds singing, and pretty flowers. Patients still enjoy these kinds of sensory experiences, but they may not be able to locate or isolate them without help (Mace 62). The best advice for teens dealing with grandmother's cognitive deficits probably comes packaged in one sentence: AD is an unpredictable illness, so one must adjust as the patient develops new symptoms (Martinson, Chesla, and Muwaswes 230).

As AD progresses, grandfather may face another frustrating symptom as his ability to communicate deteriorates. Not only does the patient lose his memory of the names of people and things, but he also loses the ability to make sense of others' words. Since reading and understanding involve two different brain functions, grandfather may be able to read the note on the refrigerator that says his lunch is in the red bowl, but he does not eat lunch because he no longer understands the meaning of the words (Mace 31). So how can young people deal with grandfather's steadily declining ability to understand and to be understood?

While very young children rarely talk about abstract topics and therefore can easily communicate with AD patients, unfortunately teens, similar to adults, frequently become angry or frustrated when grandfather can no longer speak coherently (Heston 137). Teens can best respond to communication problems with grandfather by speaking quietly and calmly; maintaining eye contact; using short, simple, familiar words and sentences; asking only one question or giving only one direction at a time; using the same words and phrasing for repeated instructions; noticing grandfather's emotions through his voice and gestures; pointing and encouraging him to point; and offering a guess when he cannot come up with a word (ADRDA, Communicating 3-5). When grandfather becomes so severely confused that he can no longer communicate, nonverbal communication, or body language, conveys more to the AD victim than words. One AD nurse suggests that teens try to enter the patient's world and become an empathetic listener, trying to identify with his feelings, needs, and emotions. For instance, in the evening, when a patient tends to wander (a symptom called "sundowners"), teens can acknowledge the wandering and try to enter the patient's world, one in which grandfather always came home from work in the evening, had supper with the family, and did outside chores. By picking up on that and talking to him about his chores, his family, his work day, a teenager helps him relax (Whyte). Holding hands, sitting beside him, and hugging are also important ways to say, "I care." Communication problems diminish, then, with careful verbal and nonverbal cues.

Perkins 5

Behavior problems, however, challenge the most tolerant families and teens. Emotional instability is one of the more common symptoms. Grandmother may yell or argue, getting easily upset seemingly over nothing (Powell 144). As one family member explained,

> The worst thing . . . is his temper. He used to be easygoing. Now he is always hollering over the least little thing. Last night he told our 10-year-old that Alaska is not a state. He was hollering and yelling and stalked out of the room. Then when I asked him to take a bath we had a real fight. He insisted he had already taken a bath (Mace 9).

Other verbal abuse may come when grandmother accuses her family of stealing her jewelry. Grandfather may insult his grandchildren by telling their friends, "They keep me prisoner in this house." Or he may direct rude remarks to their friends like, "You oughta get a haircut." Young people have difficulty dealing with this kind of socially unacceptable behavior.

The unacceptable behavior, however, is not always verbal. Teens hesitate to bring friends home because they may find grandfather sitting on the porch reading the newspaper and wearing nothing but his hat. When grandmother eats with the wrong utensils—or without utensils—teens may be repulsed. Grandfather may finally remember to dress but have his shirt buttoned incorrectly or have his sweater on backwards or inside out. When grandfather answers the phone but fails to tell his granddaughter about the young man's call, a crisis results.

To respond to such behavior problems, teens can face a real challenge. First, they should remember that, "our familiar world has become strange and perhaps threatening to the person with brain damage who cannot manage to react in an ordinary way to an ordinary situation" (Powell 159). If grandmother shouts or is angry, one must forget reasoning and logic. She cannot reason. Trying to reason with her most often leads to an argument. Instead, family members can quietly divert attention by changing the subject, looking at old photographs, or singing old songs. Even ignoring unwanted behavior works better than reacting to it (Cohen 161-162). One psychiatrist explained that families can better deal with outbursts by remembering that the "angry lashing out of a patient is displaced anger at the disease" (Untitled sidebar 14). Above all, teens need to make sure that friends understand that grandfather's illness "affects his memory of good manners [and that] the parts of the brain that make [him] behave as [he] should are also damaged" (Mace 107, 185). In short, his behavior is not anything he can control. As a result, professional caregivers tend to think of behavioral problems not as problems but as symptoms of a need or emotion. "Then we enter their world, help them relax, and thus prevent the behavior from recurring" (Whyte). Teens, however, as well as other family members, often find it difficult to distance themselves from the patient and let go of their own emotions. "The closer you are to someone, the harder it is to validate their world" (Whyte).

As a result of the victim's inability to control his or her behavior, the family, including teens, must adapt. If grandmother can no longer use a knife and fork, she may do better with finger foods (Kent 34). If grandfather can no longer handle buttons and zippers, pull-on clothing may meet his needs. If grandmother insists on sleeping with her sweater on, she is doing nothing harmful (Mace 22). An analogy might help to explain:

> It would be foolish to insist that a one-armed man eat chicken in the conventional manner, using a fork and knife. Equally foolish would be drawing the conclusion that he is totally incapable of eating chicken.... The humane approach would be to let him use his fingers or give him an adapted utensil that can be used with one hand. Either way, accommodating his deficiencies while allow him to make full use of his remaining ability. So, too, persons with Alzheimer's Disease cannot be forced into using resources that they do not have, but they can be directed toward using fully those resources that they do retain (Zgola 104).

As a teen struggles to learn to deal with a patient, she may need help with solutions. Perhaps only outsiders can really help a teen cope with the sibling-like rivalry that arises when she gives up her room, a vacation, or other material things because of a grandparent with AD (Ronch 55). Outsiders, too, can help a teen cope with the grief she feels when someone who always baked cookies for her or babysat for her is now so dramatically changed that the roles are reversed and the teen babysits the grandmother (Mace 153). Traditionally, the best help either comes from counselors or support groups.

Teens face the same range of emotions that others face, including anger, shame, self-pity, guilt, anxiety, depression, and stress (Oliver v-vi). As a result, young people need to learn everything they can so they know what is going to happen. The knowledge helps them to better handle the inevitable problems (Stolen Tomorrows). Young people also need to know that there are other teens who are living with a grandparent with AD. They also experience problems such as a lack of privacy because grandfather wanders; having to be quiet because grandmother gets excited; complaining about the way grandfather eats or acts; having to assume much more responsibility at home; and receiving less and less attention from parents who must spend more and more time taking care of grandmother (Mace 186). Teachers, other relatives, and counselors—any adult not too tired from caring for the AD victim—can help teens "who cannot understand what they interpret as a loss of interest or of love by a patient" (Cohen 214). Teens who do not get help often become "demanding and rebellious, or show violent outbursts, and generally misbehave at home and school" (Cohen 214). Thus, seeking help is best for everyone— the AD patient, parents, and teens.

Other teens may need help coping with personal fears. Some fear that AD is contagious (it is not) or fear they will inherit the illness. While certain studies do link Alzheimer's Disease to heredity (Majeski), statistics suggest that only a very small percentage of cases illustrate genetic factors. In fact, "there are several ways to get Alzheimer's: inherit one of at least four bad genes, have too little of several key brain chemicals, or at some point in life suffer damage to the tiny blood vessels that nourish the brain" ("Quietly Closing" 112). Other teens fear alienation from their friends because of a grandparent's odd, even bizarre, behavior. Some teens, however, find some comfort in the recognition that numerous celebrities have suffered from AD. ("Celebrity Victims" 626). Other teens in support groups note, when they explain to their friends that grandfather is sick, that most friends are "sympathetic and understanding once they know what [the] situation is" (ADRDA, Especially 5). Personal fears diminish with understanding.

Coping with a loved one's dementia demands every capability families can muster, but sometimes the teenager becomes the unseen victim, left to muddle through on his own. As Dr. Monica Blumenthal of the University of Pittsburgh School of Medicine said, "In many ways, dementia is like death. It is the death of the mind. Most family members who are close to the patient will go through some phase of mourning which is often more grievous than that produced by death itself, [while others call the disease] a funeral that never ends" (Leroux 4). One teenager wrote of her grandfather:

> I love you
> I hated you
> I laughed at you
> I laughed with you
> I sang with you
> I danced with you
> I talked with you
> I yelled at you
> I listened to you
> I ignored you
> and now
> I miss you (Honel 139).

Just like Lear's daughter Cordelia, teenage family members must reach for understanding and empathy. They need to understand how to respond to the debilitating illness—its cognitive degeneration, communication impairment, and behavioral symptoms. In addition, however, they also need supportive sympathy, perhaps counseling, to help them through the seeming never-ending funeral of their loved one.

Works Cited

The Alzheimer's Disease and Related Disorders Association, Inc.
Alzheimer's Disease: Especially for Teenagers. Chicago: ADRDA, 1987.

—.Alzheimer's Disease Statistics. Chicago: ADRDA, Aug. 1991.

—.Communicating with the Alzheimer Patient. Chicago: ADRDA, 1990.

"Celebrity Victims." The CQ Researcher 24 July 1992: 626.

"Chronology." The CO Researcher 24 July 1992: 625.

Cohen, Donna. The Loss of Self: A Family Resource for the Care of Alzheimer's
    Disease and Relate Disorders. New York: Norton, 1986.

Heston, Leonard L. The Vanishing Mind: A Practical Guide to Alzheimer's Disease
    and Other Dementias. New York: W. H. Freeman, 1991.

Honel, Rosalie Walsh. Journey with Grandpa: Our Family Struggle with Alzheimer's
    Disease. Baltimore: Johns Hopkins University Press, 1988.

Kent, Don. "Creating a Home That Speaks Their Language." Aging Magazine
    363-364 (1992): 32-34.

Leroux, Charles. Coping and Caring: Living with Alzheimer's Disease. Washington,
    D.C.: American Association of Retired Persons, Health Advocacy Services
    Program Department, 1986.

Mace, Nancy L. The 36-Hour Day: A Family Guide to Caring for Persons with
    Alzheimer's Disease, Related Dementing Illnesses, and Memory Loss in Later
    Life. Baltimore: Johns Hopkins University Press, 1981.

Majeski, Tom, "New Study Links Alzheimer's Disease to Heredity." St. Paul
    (Minnesota) Pioneer Press-Dispatch 19 April 1991 (Located in NewsBank
    [Microform], Health, Education and Aging, 1991, 32:E6, fiche).

Martinson, Ida M., Catherine Chesla, and Marylou Muwaswes. "Caregiving Demands
    of Patients with Alzheimer's Disease." Journal of Community Health Nursing
    October 1993: 225-232.

Oliver, Rose. Coping with Alzheimer's: A Caregiver's Emotional Survival Guide. New
    York: Dodd, Mead, 1987.

Powell, Lenore S. Alzheimer's Disease: A Guide for Families. Reading, Mass.:
    Addison-Wesley, 1983.

"Quietly Closing in on Alzheimer's." Business Week 3 May 1993: 112-113.

Ronch, Judah L. Alzheimer's Disease: A Practical Guide for Those Who Help Others.
    New York: Continuum, 1989.

Shakespeare, William. Shakespeare: Twenty-Three Plays and the Sonnets. Ed.
    Thomas Marc Parrott. Rev. ed. New York: Charles Scribner's Sons, 1953.

"Stages of Alzheimer's Disease." Aging Magazine 363-364 (1992): 16-17.

Stolen Tomorrows. Videotape. Dev. Lincoln General Hospital, Van Nuys, Calif. AIMS
    Media, 1988.26 min.

Tanner, Fredericka, and Sharon Shaw. Caring: A Family Guide to Managing the
    Alzheimer's Patient at Home. New York: New York City Alzheimer's Resource
    Center, program of New York City Department for the Aging, 1985.

Untitled sidebar. Aging Magazine 363-364 (1992): 14.

Whyte, Vickie. Dir. Alzheimer's Unit, McCurdy Healthcare Center, Evansville, Ind.
    Personal interview. 12 Aug. 1994.

You Are Not Alone. Videotape. Retirement Research Foundation Video Collection on
    Aging. Park Ridge, Ill.: Retirement Research Foundation, 1984. 28 min.

Zgola, Jitka M. Doing Things: A Guide to Programming Organized Activities for
    Persons with Alzheimer's Disease and Related Disorders. Baltimore: Johns
    Hopkins University Press, 1987.

Appendix Two

SAMPLE TABLE OF CONTENTS

SAMPLE LIST OF TABLES

Appendix Three

ABBREVIATIONS AND SYMBOLS USED IN FOOTNOTES AND BIBLIOGRAPHIES

anon.	anonymous
art., arts.	article(s)
bk., bks.	book(s)
©, c.	copyright
c., ca.	*circa* (about; approximately)
cf.	confer (compare)
ch., Chap., chs., chaps.	chapter(s)
col., cols.	column(s)
diss.	dissertation
ed., edn.	edition
ed., eds.˙	editor(s); when preceding the name, it means "edited by"
e.g.	*exempli gratia* (for example)
esp.	especially
et al.	*et alii* (and others)
f., ff.	the following page(s), e.g., p. 11f. or p.11ff.
ibid.	*ibidem* (in the same place)
i.e.	*id est* (that is)
introd.	introduction
l., ll.	line(s)
loc. cit.	*loco citato* (in the place cited)

MS., MSS., ms., mss.	manuscript(s)
N.B., n.b.	*nota bene* (note well)
n.d.	no date given
n.p.	no publisher or place of publication given
No., Nos.	number(s)
numb.	numbered
op. cit.	*opere citato* (in the work cited)
p., pp.	page(s)
passim	here and there
par., pars.	paragraph(s)
rev.	revised
sic	thus
tr., tens., trans.	translator, translated, translation
v.	*vide* (see)
vs., vss.	verse(s)
vol., vols.	volume(s)
. . .	ellipsis
/	line division in short verse quotations when not set off from text
[ ]	inclusion of editorial material within quotation